Celtic names
for CHILDREN

LORETO TODD is Reader in International English at the University of Leeds and has lectured worldwide. Educated in Northern Ireland and Leeds, she has degrees in English and Linguistics. She has written more than twenty books, including *Words Apart: A Dictionary of Northern Ireland English* and *The Language of Irish Literature* and has edited and contributed to a wide range of journals.

Celtic names

for CHILDREN

LORETO TODD

THE O'BRIEN PRESS
DUBLIN

First published 1998 by The O'Brien Press Ltd,
20 Victoria Road, Rathgar, Dublin 6, Ireland
Tel. +353 1 4923333; Fax. +353 1 4922777
email: books@obrien.ie
website: http://www.obrien.ie

ISBN: 0-86278-556-1

British Library Cataloguing-in-Publication Data
A cataloguing reference for this title is available
from the British Library

2   3   4   5   6   7   8   9   10
98   99   00   01   02   03   04   05   06   07

The O'Brien Press receives assistance from
The Arts Council/An Chomhairle Ealaíon

Typesetting, layout, design: The O'Brien Press Ltd.
Index: Muire Spring
Cover illustration: Nicola Emoe
Cover separations: Lithoset Ltd.
Printing: Cox & Wyman Ltd.

CONTENTS

NOTE: Where an index entry is followed by more than one page number, the first number indicates the most comprehensive reference.

The Celts

The Celts were once found all over Europe, from the Black Sea in the east to Ireland in the west, from south-west Spain and southern Italy through Switzerland and up as far north as Denmark. The Greeks called them *Keltoi* and evidence of their existence can be traced back to the fifth century BC. The Celts were known by different names in different areas: *Galli* or *Gauls* in France and parts of Italy, *Galatae* in the Balkans and Asia Minor, *Celtiberi* in Spain.

Apart from inscriptions found in various parts of Europe, most of our knowledge of the Celtic family of languages comes from what has become known as *Insular Celtic*, that is, the name given to the varieties found in Brittany and the British Isles.

Insular Celtic seems to have reached western Europe in two waves. The Goidelic (later Gaelic) Celts reached Ireland around the fourth century BC and this form of Celtic spread to the Isle of Man and Scotland. A second group, the Brythonic Celts, conquered and settled in parts of England, including Cornwall and Devon, and into Wales and Brittany.

These groups spoke different varieties of Celtic. The Goidelic speakers are sometimes referred to as the Q-Celts and the Brythonic groups as P-Celts because certain words began with a sound that was represented by 'q' (later 'c') in Goidelic and with a 'p' in Brythonic. Thus, where modern Irish Gaelic now has *ceann* and *ceathair* for 'head' and 'four', Welsh has *penn* and *pedwar*.

The Celtic languages have all suffered serious decline, especially since the seventeenth century. The last mother-tongue speakers of Cornish died in the nineteenth century; the last mother-tongue speaker of Manx Gaelic in the 1970s. There are perhaps a million people who know some Breton but only a fraction of this number speak it fluently. Another two million speakers know Gaelic, in its Irish, Scottish and Cape Breton (Nova Scotian) forms, but perhaps only 200,000 speak it regularly and for most purposes. Welsh is probably the most vital of the Celtic languages, having as many as half a million regular users, including some speakers in Patagonia (Argentina) where 150 Welsh people settled in 1865.

Naming

Worldwide, naming has always been culturally significant and we often assume, incorrectly, that the system of first name(s) followed by a surname is universal. Surnames tend to be placed first in China and West Africa where, for example, *Djou Dun Ren* or *Mbagwa Mary* would be referred to in English as *Mr Djou* and *Mrs Mbagwa*. Surnames were not universal in the Celtic-speaking communities until the nineteenth century when *Ap* and *Mac* meaning 'son' were often used so that, in Wales, the son of Harry or Hugh might have become *Ap + Harry* or *Ap + Hugh*, resulting in the blends *Parry* and *Pugh*. In Ireland, only the prefixes *Mac* (son) and *Ó* (descendant) are widespead, although the feminine form *Ní*, or *Nic* (daughter), is occasionally used as in *Siubhan Ní Dhuibhir* (daughter of *Duibhir*).

In choosing a child's first name, parents often say something about their hopes, their dreams, their aspirations. Sometimes, there is an association with God, as in the Hebrew *Samuel* (asked of God), or the Greek *Dorothy* (gift of God); often there is a link with love, as in the French-derived *Amy* (loved one), the Latin *Alma* (loving, kind), or the Lamso *Bongcong* (it is good to love). Parents have found inspiration, especially for their daughters, in nature, *Daisy*, *Fern* and *Hyacinth*; in jewels, *Beryl*, *Jade* and *Pearl*; in months of the year, such as *Avril*, *April*, *May* and *June*; and they have perhaps indulged in wishful thinking in the selection of virtues such as *Constance*, *Felicity* or *Prudence*. The spectrum of colours has provided *Blanche* (white), *Rory* (red) and *Suneel* (dark blue); places have given us *Francis* (man of France), *Kirk* (near the church) or *Neville* (new town); and aspects of warfare have provided a range of names, especially for sons, including *Alexander* (defender), *Edgar* (rich spear) and *Finlay* (fair-haired warrior).

The Celts, like all other groups of people, took care to pick the appropriate name for their children. *Glenys* meant 'holy', *Phelim* suggested 'always good' and *Tristram* implied 'hero'. As the Celtic languages were over-run by stronger neighbours, Breton names were often replaced by French forms and Welsh, Cornish and Gaelic names gave way to English ones. Recently, however, people of Celtic origin, and people who are interested in Celtic culture, have sought out the given names of their ancestors and have reintroduced names such as *Angharad* (really loved), *Ceridwen* (fair poetry), *Cillian* (little church), *Cormac* (son of the raven) and *Demelza* and *Denzel* (Cornish placenames). It is, perhaps, their way of saying: 'I may no longer speak my Celtic language but I'm a Celt or I'm pro-Celt and proud to be so.'

Spelling and pronunciation

Many names have several spellings and a variety of pronunciations. The Irish forms of Catherine and John, for example, may occur as *Caitlín*, *Caitlin*, *Caitríona*, *Cathleen*, *Kathleen*, *Caitlin* may be pronounced as 'kotch + leen' or 'kot + leen' or 'koit +leen' or 'kate + leen' or 'kate + linn' and John as *Seán*, or *Séan*, *Shaun*, *Shawn* or *Shane*. And these are the easy ones! Even within Ireland, there were several dialects, each with its own sound preferences; each with its own pet forms; some using a length mark or *fada*; others leaving the vowel unmarked. In addition, many of the names were recorded in Latin or French or English as well as Irish, thus providing a wide range of choice for parents and a nightmare for the dictionary maker. Some names have been adopted – and adapted – worldwide. Kevin, for example has travelled widely from its origin as *Caoimhín* (beautiful birth) and was, for example, one of the ten most popular names for African American boys in 1982.

The system employed in this book is relatively straightforward. The main entry is found under the most frequently-used spelling; variants are provided and the most widely used pronunciation supplied. Where the 'same' name may begin with a different letter, as with *Hamish* and *Seamus*, two entries are provided.

The Future

It is often said that the Chinese had a proverb which translates roughly as: 'It is incredibly difficult to predict, especially with regard to the future.' Underneath this truism, there is a grain of truth. It is extraordinarily hard to know what the future holds. Four hundred years ago, few people would have guessed that the English language would be the most widely-spoken language the world has ever known. Ten years ago, even fewer would have predicted the role of the worldwide web in education. None of us can be certain what will happen to people or to languages. It is even possible that the decline suffered by the Celtic languages will be reversed. Be that as it may, however, we are on safer ground in predicting that the current interest in all things Celtic will grow. More and more people will seek out the names associated with their roots and resonant names such as *Caradoc* and *Cliona*, *Dewi* and *Dympna*, *Enid* and *Ethna*, *Glyn* and *Gobnaid* may become as popular as *Conor* and *Niamh* currently are in parts of Northern Ireland.

Many people will continue the practice of using a Celtic surname such as *Dillon*, *Donnellan*, *Morgan* and *Murphy* as first names. These feel right as first names because that's what they were originally. Others will search out meanings and forms that are beautiful and give these as gifts to their children. Among this list, we might suggest *Aibreán* (April), *Áilghean* (gentle), *Airgead* (silver) for girls and *Aimsitheoir* (marksman, discover), *Airdeall* (watchfulness) or *Anamchara* (spiritual helper) for boys.

And, if you read this book when your child-naming days are over, let me provide an alternative. Would you not think of naming your dog *Mící* or your cat *Pangur*? Certainly, if you chose the latter, you would be in a noble tradition of naming. Over one thousand years ago, a medieval word processor, that is, a monk, scribbled a poem on the edge of his vellum:

Messe ocus Pangur bán	Me and white Pangur
cechtar nathar fria saindán	practise both our art
bíth a menmasam fri seilgg	his mind is on hunting
mu menma céin im saincheirdd.	my own mind on my craft.

Every time I see a white cat, I think of this nameless scribe. Naming a cat has given them both a form of immortality.

GIRLS' NAMES

Aamor (pronounced like 'ah + more'), **Aenor, Alienor**
The Breton name Aamor has several variants, including Aenor and Alienor. Although it was originally a form of Helen, possibly from Greek *helios*, 'sun' and thus meaning 'sun-beam', it has taken on some of the associations of Latin *amor*, 'love', and is now often linked with warmth and affection.

Adaryn, Aderyn (pronounced like 'add + er + in')
This Welsh name comes from Welsh *aderyn*, meaning 'bird', and suggests a person who is not held back by earthly restrictions or limitations.

Adigis (pronounced like 'add + aegis')
This Cornish name belonged to a duchess whose daughter was St Sererena. It may be related to Welsh *addolgar*, 'devout'.

Ado (pronounced like 'add + oh')
A pet form of the Cornish name Gunoda, which is related to Welsh Gwynneth, meaning 'blessed'.
SEE: **Gunoda, Gwyneth**

Aela (pronounced like 'ale + a')
This Breton name is the feminine form of Ael and seems to be related to words for 'ardour' or 'rampart'.
SEE: **Ael**

Aenor
SEE: **Aamor**

Aerona, Aeronwen
Both of these names come from the Welsh noun *areon*, meaning 'berries'. The tradition of calling children after flowers, plants and naturally occurring phenomena is found in all of the Celtic languages.

Afton
Afton is the name of a river in Scotland, immortalised by Rabbie Burns in:

> Flow gently, sweet Afton, among thy green braes;
> Flow gently, I'll sing thee a song in thy praise.

Afton has been taken over as a girl's name, suggesting 'one from Afton'. An old Gaelic plural of *abha*, 'river', was *aibhnte*, a form that is close to Afton.

Africa, Africah
Records suggest that a twelfth-century queen of the Isle of Man was called Africa or Africah. This name was certainly inspired by the continent but probably reinforced by the Gaelic word *fioreach*, meaning 'noble'.

Aibhlínn, Eibhlínn (pronounced like 'I've + leen')
It seems likely that the Normans took the name Aveline to Britain and Ireland. It developed several forms, including Aibhilín, Eveleen, Eveline, Evelyn and Evelyne. The name Aveline probably means 'longed-for child' and it may be the partial source of Ava.
SEE: **Éibhlean**

Aibreán, Aibreann (pronounced like 'ab + rawn')
This is the Gaelic form of the month 'April' and is sometimes used as a girl's name. The name was borrowed from Latin *Aprilis* but goes back to Etruscan and seems to have been associated with Spring. The Welsh equivalent is Ebrill.

Aideen (pronounced like 'ay + deen')
Aideen is related to Aedh and Aidan in its meaning of 'fire'. The Gaelic word *adughadh* means 'act of igniting, kindling'. Aideen was the wife of Oscar, a grandson of Fionn MacCool. Like many Celtic women, she was capable of loving only one man, and when Oscar was killed in battle she died of a broken heart.

Aifric (pronounced like 'aff + rick')
This form of Africa has been used in Scotland. It is the Gaelic from of 'Africa' and is an attractive variant.

Aileen, Ailene (pronounced like 'ay + leen')
These are two of the many variants of Helen found in Ireland, Scotland and the Isle of Man. Helen comes from Greek *helios*, 'sun', and suggests 'sunbeam, ray of sunshine'. Like Eileen, they are forms of the Greek name, Helen, the beautiful woman for whom the Trojan War was fought.
SEE: **Aleine, Eileen, Lena**

Ailis, Ailish (pronounced like 'ale + ish' or 'isle + ish')

This is the Irish form of a name which was brought to Ireland by the Normans in such forms as Alice, rhyming with 'palace', and Alicia. The name is probably a variant of Adelaide, coming from Germanic *adal*, 'noble, well born' and *heid*, 'kind'. It is becoming popular again. Alice la Beale (Alice the Beautiful), a contemporary of King Arthur, had her face covered by a veil so that people would not die at the sight of her extraordinary beauty.
SEE: **Éilis**

Ailsa (pronounced like 'ale + sa')
This Scottish name is probably derived from the island Ailsa Craig or 'rock island', which is in the Firth of Clyde. Calling children after places is not uncommon. We find it with Florence and Lourdes as well as Kerry and Tyrone. The island's name may mean 'eagle rock'. Its use as a girl's name is probably due to the -a ending, increasingly thought of as feminine. In Gaelic, however, the -a ending could occur in names for both men and women. Cúchulainn's real name, for example, was Setanta, and the mother of Conchubar, the king of Ulster, was Nessa.

Áine, Annie (pronounced to rhyme with 'awe' + the ending 'nia' of 'Sonia')
Most people assume that this is an Irish form of Anne or Hannah, meaning 'God has favoured me', but it is, in fact, an old Irish name meaning 'brightness, luminosity' and

could originally be used for either a male or a female. Gaelic also has a noun *áine*, implying 'delight, agility, melody' and these meanings have reinforced the popularity of the name. Áine may have been a fertility goddess. She was traditionally associated with generosity and Áines are supposed to be lucky in love and with money.

Because Áine is regarded as a form of Anne, the name is associated with St Anne, the mother of Mary, and the grandmother of Jesus. Her feast day is 26 July. The form Annie occurs in Gaelic areas as a halfway house between Gaelic Áine and English Anne.

SEE: **Enya**

Aingeal (pronounced like 'ang + ell')
This name is the Gaelic equivalent of 'angel' and comes from Greek *angelos*, meaning 'divine messenger'. The English equivalent is Angela; Angelique is found in Brittany and Angyles has been recorded for Wales.

Ainslee, Ainsley, Ainslie

Ainsley was originally most frequently found in Scotland but is now popular in many English-speaking communities. It is probable that the first syllable comes from Gaelic *aon*, meaning 'one', and that the second syllable may be from *laoi*, 'poem', influenced by the English '-ley', 'meadow', as in Ilkley or Otley.

Aislin, Aislinn, Aisling, Ashling (pronounced like 'ash + ling')

Derives from the Gaelic word *aisling* 'dream, vision' and has become popular in Ireland, England and the US. Although the name could logically be used of either sex, its modern use is restricted to girls. Part of the explanation for this lies in the type of vision described by the word *aisling*. A dreamer sees a beautiful woman who belongs to the spirit world, and when he wakes up he can never again be content. Keats's poem 'La Belle Dame Sans Merci' may have been influenced by an *aisling* story:

> I met a lady in the meads,
> Full beautiful – a faery's child,
> Her hair was long, her foot was light,
> And her eyes were wild.

Alana, Alanna, Alannah (pronounced like 'al + an + na')

This name derives from the Gaelic term of endearment *a leanbh* (child), although it is sometimes thought to be the feminine form of *Alan* and is found in all parts of the Celtic world. The term *a leanbh* was pronounced 'alanna' and is often translated as 'darling' to indicate its warmth. Lana is probably a derived name.

Aleine (pronounced to rhyme with 'a + lane')

This form of Helen, meaning 'sunbeam', is sometimes written Eleyne. It was the name of Sir Gawain's niece. Aleine loved Sir

Perceval and was instrumental in his becoming a Knight of the Round Table.

SEE: **Aileen**

Alienor

SEE: **Aamor**

Almeda

This Breton name is becoming popular, especially for girls born in August. It is possible that it is a modified form of Latin *alma*, 'kind', influenced by *amanda*, 'worthy of love'. There is also a Latin word *almeda*, meaning 'clearly focused, goal-oriented'.

Almha, Alva, Alvag (pronounced like 'Alva')

Almha was an Irish goddess renowned for her strength and prowess. The meaning of the name is not certain although it may be a form of *albha*, 'medication'. It seems to have been influenced by Latin *alma*, 'kind, nourishing', found most frequently in the phrase *alma mater* (benign mother). The Breton name *Almeda* is not directly related but is an attractive alternative.

Amena, Amina, Amine

These variants are from a Celtic root meaning 'honest, utterly pure'. They are similar to the Arabic name Amena, meaning 'aspiration', and may also have been influenced by Amen, meaning 'so be it'.

Anchoret (pronounced like 'an + hor + it')

This attractive Welsh name derives from *cariad*, 'love' and means 'greatly loved'.

SEE: **Angharad**

Andrea

SEE: **Andrew**

Aneira

Aneira is related to the Welsh noun *anrhydedd*, meaning 'honour'.

SEE: **Annowre**

Angharad (pronounced like 'an + har + rid')

Angharad is probably related to both *cariad*, 'love' and *cerydd*, 'reproach' and suggests 'without reproach'. The name was popular in the Middle Ages, then virtually died out in Wales, before being revived in the twentieth century.

SEE: **Anchoret**

Annowre (pronounced like 'an + our + ri')

It is not certain what Annowre means. It may be related to Aneurin, which is thought to come from Latin *honorius;* Annowre would thus mean 'honoured woman'. Annowre seems to have loved King Arthur and to have lured him into the forest. When he resisted her charms, she was angered and tried to steal the sword, Excalibur, so that Arthur would be as vulnerable as any mortal man.

SEE: **Aneira**

Aobh, Aoibh (pronounced like 'eve' or 'ave')

Aobh's name comes from Gaelic

aobh, meaning 'beauty, radiance', and she was the first wife of King Lír and the mother of the four children who were turned into swans by Lír's second wife. The name is frequently equated with the biblical Eve, which probably comes from Hebrew *chava*, 'life'.

SEE: **Aoife**

Aobhnaid, Aobhnait

(pronounced like 'eve + nidge' or 'eve + nitch')

SEE: **Aoibheann**

Aodhnard, Aodhnart

SEE: **Enat**

Aoibheann, Aoibhinn

(pronounced like 'ay + von', 'eve + een' or 'eve +in')

This name is often interpreted as 'little Eve'. It comes, however, from Irish Gaelic *aoibhinn*, meaning 'of radiant beauty', and has a related form in Aobhnaid or Aobhnait. The name is sometimes anglicised as Eavan, as in the name of a contemporary Irish poet, Eavan Boland.

SEE: **Aobh, Aobhnaid, Aobhnait, Aoife, Eavan**

Aoibhel(l) (pronounced like 'ee + fell')

This name comes from *aoibheall*, meaning 'joyful, beautiful'. Aoibhel was an Irish spirit woman who played the harp so beautifully that anyone who heard the music died from utter joy.

Aoife (pronounced like 'eef + a')

Aoife is related to Aoibheann. It means 'radiance, joy' and is often used as the Irish equivalent of 'Eve', which probably comes from a Hebrew noun *chava*, meaning 'life'. The name is experiencing renewed popularity and in 1997, for example, Siamese twin girls named Aoife and Niamh made the headlines when they were successfully separated.

One of the earliest records of the name comes from a story about Cúchulainn. Aoife was a Scottish warrior queen and the mother of Cúchulainn's son. Another Aoife was reputed to be the second wife of King Lír and the woman who turned his children into swans. Ava may be a related form.

Aouregwenn (pronounced to rhyme with 'a + oor + gwen')

This Breton name seems to be derived from a Celtic word similar to Welsh *gwyn*, 'white, pure, fair'. The final syllable reminds us of the closeness between Breton and Welsh.

SEE: **Gwen**

Ardanata

Ardanata may not be a Celtic name but a beautiful maiden with this name occurs in Welsh legends. The name may, however, be related to Gaelic *árduighte*, 'exalted, honoured'.

Argante (pronounced like 'are + gant + ti')

Argante was a Celtic goddess of the

Underworld, a place of joy and celebration, utterly unlike Hell. Her name may be derived from a Latin word *argentum*, meaning 'silver', or it may be a form of Morgan le Faye.

Arianrhod

Arianrhod is a Welsh goddess figure whose name is associated with the star constellation Corona Borealis, and may mean 'silver wheel'. The Welsh word for 'silver' is *ariannaid*. She attempts to prove her virginity by walking over the wand of Math, a god who will die if he cannot rest his feet in the lap of a virgin. As she steps over the wand, Arianrhod becomes pregnant and gives birth to twins, Dylan and Llew.

Arlen, Arlena, Arlene, Arlène

These are probably derived from the French place Arles, although they may also derive from Celtic words meaning 'binding promise after consultation'. Welsh, for example has *addewid*, 'promise', and Gaelic had *airle*, 'consultation'. The name is found in France as Arlène.

Armelle

It seems likely that Armelle comes from Brittany, where it is said to mean 'high ranking lady, princess'. There are many possible Celtic source words for this name. Gaelic, for example, has *áirmeach*, 'famous, splendid'.

Athracht, Attracta (pronounced like 'a + troct' or 'a + track + ta')

Many people have assumed that Attracta comes from the Latin verb *attrahere*, meaning 'draw towards, attract', and it is likely that this meaning has contributed to its use. A form of the name occurs, however, in sixth-century Ireland as that of one of a number of female saints who gave up a life of comparative luxury for one of dedication. Athracht may, therefore come from a Gaelic noun *athrach*, 'change, alteration'. The early Irish Christians tried to change their ways and live in the poverty and simplicity advocated by Christ. They had few clothes and even fewer possessions, their churches were small and spare and they channelled all their love of art and colour and music into their illuminated manuscripts and liturgical chants.

Aude (pronounced like 'aud' or 'ode')

The name Aude occurs both in Brittany and in Cornwall, where a saint of this name was beheaded in the tenth or eleventh century. It is uncertain what Aude means but it seems to be related to Gunoda and thus to mean 'blessed'. A story about the Breton princess, Aude the Fair, is told in the medieval romance *Chanson de Roland*. Aude, like many Celtic women, loved one man so completely that no-one could ever replace him. She was betrothed to Roland but Charlemagne decided he wanted her as a wife for his son, Louis. He told Aude that Roland was dead but that his son would be her husband. Aude replied that, if Roland was dead, the earth had no more attractions for her and she fell dead at Charlemagne's feet.

SEE: **Gunoda**

Ava

SEE: **Aibhlín, Aoife**

Awena

This Welsh name comes from *awen*, 'muse', and suggests 'poetic, inspirer of poetry'.

Azenor (pronounced like 'as + a + nor')

Azenor was a beautiful Breton princess who was unjustly accused of adultery. She was sealed in a barrel and set adrift on the sea where her son, Budoc, was born. The barrel was washed up on the Irish coast where Azenor and her son were welcomed. It is not certain what the name comes from although it may be related to *aisnéis*, 'testimony, evidence'.

Baibín (pronounced like 'bah + been'), Bairbín, Báirbre (pronounced like 'bar + breh'), Barba, Barbara, Barbra

The Greek name *barbara* meant 'foreign woman' and it was adopted into Latin as a woman's name, Barbara. A similar adoption can be seen with the name 'Wallace', which comes from an Old English adjective *wealh*, meaning 'foreign'. The Celts adopted this name because of the popularity of the legend of St Barbara. She was executed by her father because she refused to give up her attachment to Christianity. He was punished by being struck by a bolt of lightning. Barbara thus became the patron saint of fireworks and artillery, as well as of stone masons and architects. (Her father was reputed to have been in a high tower when the lightning struck.) In Gaelic-speaking communities, Barbara was sometimes equated with Gobnait, possibly because of a supposed connection between the name Gobnait and the Gaelic word *gaibhneach*, meaning 'metalwork'.

SEE: **Gobnait**

Banba, Banbha (pronounced like 'ban + bah', 'ban + vah')

Banba is believed to have been one of the first settlers in Ireland. It is not clear what her name means but it is associated with *bean*, meaning 'woman' and so has similar implications to the biblical 'Eve'. There is a legend about Ireland having been at one time a country inhabited only by women, *Tír na mBan*, with Banba as their queen. Stories about islands populated entirely by women were not uncommon in Gaelic tradition. Maeldun and his followers also found such an island in their *Immrama* (journey by sea).

SEE: **Bran, Maeldún**

Beara (pronounced like 'bar + a' or
'bear + a'), **Beare**

Beara was a Celtic princess whose
name probably means 'plan, opinion',
as in modern Irish *barúil*. She
married a man who had been
transformed into a salmon, but her
love for him, even in this form, helped
to set him free.

Bec, Becca

This name derives from a Gaelic
adjective *beag* meaning 'small'. Bec
was a goddess who guarded the Well
of Knowledge and Wisdom. This
name is also used as an abbreviation
of Rebecca, which has been popular
in a variety of forms in Celtic areas at
least as far back as the sixteenth
century.

Becuma

Becuma was a spirit woman whose
name may be associated with bees.
The Gaelic word for 'bee-keeper' is
beachaire. Or it may come from *bean
+ uaigneach*, meaning 'lonely
woman'. Becuma fell in love with Art
but married his father, Conn of the
Hundred Battles, because she
thought that power lasted longer than
love. When Conn died, Art took over
the kingdom of Tara and banished
Becuma.

Bedelia

Bedelia may be a form of Bríd and
may have been influenced by
brígheúil, meaning 'mighty, powerful'. It is also possible that it is a
blend of Bríd and Celia, which is

related to Latin *caelum*, 'heaven', and
implies 'heavenly'.
SEE: **Delia**

Béibhinn (pronounced like 'bay + veen'), **Bevan, Bevin, Vivanne, Vivian, Vivien, Vivienne**

This name is almost certainly a blend
of *bean*, 'woman', and *finn* or *fionn*
'fair', and the term may originally
have been applied to Viking women.
Certainly, it was the given name of
the mother and daughter of Brian
Boru, the Irish king who expelled the
Danes at the Battle of Clontarf in
1014. An earlier reference to the
name goes back to Irish mythology,
where a tall Béibhinn sought the
protection of Fionn MacCool so that
she would not have to marry a giant.
Because the vocative form of
Béibhinn would be pronounced
'Vayveen', the name was associated
with the Norman Vivian, meaning
'alive, living'.

Benalban, Benally, Benvon, Benvy

These names are thought to be
compounds involving Gaelic *bean*,
ben meaning 'woman' and places of
origin. The four names above are
the equivalent of 'woman of
Scotland', 'woman of Ulster',
'woman of Munster' and 'woman of
Meath'.

Berc'hed

This is the Breton equivalent of Bríd
and means 'power'. Forms of this

name are found throughout the Celtic region.

SEE: **Bríd**

Beriana, Bberion, Buryan

This Cornish name is found in a variety of forms partly because, like all saints, her name is often given in Latin, and partly because a regular spelling system is a relatively modern phenomenon. Her name may mean 'gift' and so be related to Gaelic *beir*. Beriana is reputed to have cured a prince who was paralysed. In a twelfth-century list of Cornish saints, it is claimed that Beriana came from Ireland, but it is more likely that she was either Cornish or Breton. Irish saints were held in such high esteem throughout the Celtic world that it was almost traditional to claim that a saint was born in Ireland.

Berneen

This attractive Irish name may be a diminutive of Bernadette and would thus mean 'hardy little bear'. Bernadette and Berneen both come from the Germanic combination *bern* + *hard*, 'hardy bear'. The Irish *-ín* is a diminutive marker.

Bethan, Betha, Beatha

(pronounced like 'ba +ha')

There are three possible sources for these names. They may be a blend of (Eliza)beth + Anne, Hebrew names meaning 'God is my oath' and 'God has favoured me'. They may possibly be a reduction of the Hebrew Bethany, meaning 'house of dates' and reputed to be the place where Mary, Martha and Lazarus lived (Luke, 19: 29). They may also be from the Gaelic word *beatha*, meaning 'life'. The name of the Scottish king Macbeth certainly means 'son of life'.

Bevan, Bevin

SEE: **Béibhinn**

Blaine, Blayne

Blaine is probably from a Gaelic word *bléan* meaning 'narrow, hollow'. It may also mean 'white, fair' and come from *bléin-fhinne*, 'whiteness'.

Bláithín (pronounced like 'blah + heen'), **Blaithnéid** (pronounced like 'blaw + nade'), **Bláthnaid** (pronounced like 'blaw + nid), **Blathnait** (pronounced like 'blaw it'), **Blanaid** (pronounced like 'blaw + nidge')

These names are all variants of the Gaelic noun *bláth*, meaning 'flower'. They are sometimes translated as Blossom. The custom of naming a girl after a flower or a plant can be seen in such names as Daisy, Fern, Heather, and Primrose. The Irish Bláthnaid fell in love with Cúchulainn and helped him to defeat her husband so that they would be free to marry.

SEE: **Blodwen**

Blinne, Blinnie (pronounced like 'blin + nih'), Bluinse

The Irish saint Blinne, whose name seems to mean 'noble', is also known as Monenna. Blinne probably lived in the fifth century and she is said to have been a friend of St Brigid. Blinne may also mean 'fair-skinned' because Blinne, Blinnie and Bluinse were medieval abbreviations of Blanche, the French feminine form of 'white'.

SEE: **Mona, Monenna**

Blodeuwedd (pronounced like 'blod + doo + widh')

This Welsh name is like Gaelic Bláthnaid in being related to 'flower'. Welsh *blodyn* means 'flower, blossom'. Legend suggests that Blodeuwedd was created from flowers as a bride for Llew of the Dextrous Hand but that she fell in love with a hunter and sought to kill Llew. As a punishment, she was transformed into an owl.

Blodwen

Blodwen is a compound of Welsh *blodyn*, meaning 'flower', and *gwyn*, meaning 'white, holy'. The name is thus similar in form and meaning to Gaelic Bláthnaid. These Celtic names may also have increased the popularity of Blanche, meaning 'white', in Brittany. The sound of Blanche overlaps that of Bláthnaid and the meaning overlaps Blodwen.

Bluinse
SEE: **Blinne**

Boadicea (pronounced like 'boa + diss + ee + a'), **Boudicca** (pronounced like 'boo + dick + ah')

We are not certain what Boadicea's name means but it is probably related to *buaidh*, 'victory'. When the Romans invaded Britain, the entire island was Celtic. The queen of the Iceni, a tribe in the south of the country, was Boudicca, latinised as Boadicea. When the Romans attempted to annex her kingdom, she led a rebellion against them in AD 61. She forced their surrender in several areas but was eventually captured. To avoid the humiliation of being paraded in Rome, she is said to have committed suicide. The name is Buddug in modern Welsh.

Boann (pronounced like 'bo + an')

Boann, whose name includes *bó*, meaning 'cow', was a goddess after whom the River Boyne is named. It is possible that she was an original mother god figure associated with food and fertility. The Boyne has been significant in modern Irish history because in 1690 William III's army defeated the forces of the Catholic king, James II, at the Battle of the Boyne.

Bonnie, Bonny

In Scotland and parts of Northern Ireland, the adjective 'bonnie', which derives from French *bon*, *bonne*, 'good', means 'pretty, attractive'. It is sometimes used as a name, partly perhaps as a result of the popularity of Margaret Mitchell's novel *Gone with the Wind* and of the film based on it: the nickname of Scarlett O'Hara's daughter was Bonnie.

Brangaine (pronounced like 'brang + gy + in + na')

The Gaelic name Brangaine resembles the Welsh Brongwyn, which is made up of *bron* + *gwen* and implies 'fair beauty'. Brangaine's name may also be related to *brionglán*, 'beam'. She was the handmaiden of Iseult (also known as Isolde and Yseult). She gave Iseult and Tristan a love potion that caused them to love each other for all eternity.

Brangwyn, Branwen
SEE: **Brongwyn**

Branna, Brannagh (pronounced like 'bran + na')

Branna may be the female equivalent of Celtic *bran*, meaning 'raven' and found in some form in all of the Celtic-using communities. It may also be a variant pronunciation of Brenna or a derived form of the surname Brannagh.
SEE: **Brenna**

Branwen

This name is more usually spelt Brongwyn or Bronwen and means 'fair beauty' or 'white breast'.
SEE: **Brongwyn**

Breage, Breagg

These are variant forms of a Cornish saint who was a patron saint of midwives. The name seems to come from an adjective *breagh*, meaning 'fine, lovely'.

Bree, Breeanne, Brianne (pronounced like 'bree' and 'bree + anne')

This name may be related to Bríd, who was a Celtic goddess whose name, in the form of *brighid*, came to mean 'beautiful maiden'. The form Breeanne may be a blend of Bree and Anne or a feminine form of Brian, meaning 'eminence'.
SEE: **Bríd**

Breege (pronounced like 'breej')
SEE: **Bríd**

Breegeen (pronounced like 'bree + jean')

This name means 'little Bríd'.
SEE: **Bríd**

Brenda

Until this century, the name Brenda was virtually unknown outside Scotland. It is often thought to be the female form of Brendan, a name that may come from Welsh *brenhinol*, meaning 'royal'. It is possible that Brenda comes from Brendan, who was one of the most popular saints of the Middle Ages; it is also possible that the name is a modified form of Viking *brand*, meaning 'bright sword'.

Brenna

It is not easy to say whether Brenna is a form of Brenda, or a female form of Bran, or a form of Brynna, a female form of Welsh *bryn*, meaning 'hill'. It has been suggested that Brenna or *breana* is a name in its own right meaning 'beauty with hair as dark as a raven'.

SEE: **Branna, Bran**

Briallen

Briallen is a Welsh floral name. It is taken over from *briallen*, the word for 'primrose'. The Irish equivalent is *buidheachán*.

Briana, Bryana, Bryna (pronounced like 'bree + an + na')

These are feminine forms of Brian and mean 'noble, virtuous'.

Bríd (pronounced 'breej'), Bride, Bridie, Brídín (pronounced 'bree + jean), Bregeen, Bridget, Bridgeteen, Brighid, Brigid, Brigit, Brigiteen, Brigitte, Bree, Breda, Breege, Berc'hed, Biddie, Biddy, Birgitta

With the exception of names derived from Maria, no female name was more widely used in Celtic communities than Bríd. It seems likely that Bríd was a Celtic goddess, possibly of agriculture and healing, possibly of poetry and fire and sometimes known as 'Brigid of the Holy Fire'. Her name is related to the noun *brígh*, meaning 'power, strength, vigour, virtue'. Many of the attributes of the goddess were applied to St Brigid of Kildare who died during the first quarter of the sixth century and who is reputed to be buried in Downpatrick, in the same grave as St Patrick and St Colmcille. St Brigid was often referred to as the 'Mary of the Gael' and her feast day on 1 February coincides with the Feast of Candles, itself possibly a relic of the celebration of the victory of light over darkness. This name was so frequently given to Irish girls that 'Biddie' was used to imply any Irish girl, and many girls who went as maids to America were automatically called Biddie or Biddy.

Brisen

Brisen was a magician whose name may be related to Welsh *brenhines*, meaning 'queen'. She encouraged Lancelot to visit Elaine, who subsequently gave birth to Galahad, the noblest and purest of the Knights of the Round Table.

Brittany, Brittney

It is not unusual for placenames to be given to daughters. Often, it is cities, as with Lagos, but occasionally it is counties as with Kerry, islands as with Iona, or regions like Brittany. Brittany is the English name for the part of France that the Bretons call *Breiz* and the French call *Bretagne*. The Latin, French and Breton names come from a Celtic root that is also found in the words Britain, Briton and British.

Brollachan (pronounced like 'broll + ach + hawn')

Brollachan is a spirit figure found only in the Highlands of Scotland. She has a mouth and a pair of eyes but no tangible body, although she can adopt any form she chooses. Her name is linked to the Gaelic word *brollach*, 'breast, front of the body'.

Brona (pronounced like 'bro + nah'), Brónagh, Brónach
(pronounced l ike 'bro + nock')

The Gaelic adjective *brónach* means 'sad, sorrowful' and could, at one stage, be used as a name for either a girl or a boy. The meaning has limited the appeal of this name just as the labelling of Deirdre as 'Deirdre of the Sorrows' has reduced the popularity of Deirdre.

Brongwyn, Bronwen, Bronwyn, Brangwyn, Branwen
(pronounced like 'brong + win')

This Welsh name, which occurs in a variety of forms, derives from *bron + gwen*, meaning 'breast' + 'fair, pure, white' and was once given as a mark of respect to someone who was either physically or spiritually beautiful. One Bronwen was given in marriage to an Irish king but was so unhappy that she trained a bird to carry a message to her brother, Bran. He led a fleet across the Irish Sea to rescue her.

Brynna, Bryony

It is not certain where these names originated. Brynna may be a feminine form of Welsh Bryn, meaning 'hill', and Bryony may be a variant of this, possibly influenced by the name of the plant *brionia*.

 C

Caera, Ceara (pronounced like 'care + a')

Caera seems to come from a Gaelic word *cearbh*, meaning 'sharp, spear-like', 'desire'. This may not sound particularly appropriate for a little girl, but 'spear' could mean 'in a direct line on the father's side'. In addition, it is similar in form to Cara, meaning 'friend, loved one'.

Caer Ibormeith, Caeribormeith
(pronounced like 'kar + ee + bor + may(th)')

Caer Ibormeith was a goddess who could take on many different shapes. According to legend, she lived half of her life as a swan and half as a beautiful maiden. The form of her name suggests a Welsh origin with a meaning related to *caer*, 'fortress,' but, according to an early Irish manuscript, Aengus saw her in a dream and would have died of love if he had not found her. An Irish origin may be found in *cearbh mór*, 'great desire'.

Cairenn (pronounced like 'care + in'), Caryn, Karen, Karin, Karel, Keren

Cairenn was the mother of the legendary Niall of the Nine Hostages and the concubine of King Eochu. Her name seems to come from *cara + -ín*, meaning 'little beloved' and, although it may be pronounced like Karen or Karin, it is not a borrowing from the Viking languages or an Irish form of Katherine. Cairenn was treated harshly by Eochu's wife, but a poet fostered her son until he could claim his inheritance. When Niall was king, he treated Cairenn with great love and reverence. Irish tradition states that she was a British slave so her name may be from the Latin Carina. The name Karen and a variant Karel are found in Brittany.

Caitlín (pronounced like 'kotch + leen' or 'koit + leen' but as 'kate + lynn' in America), **Caitlin, Cathleen, Cathline, Katelin, Kaytlin, Kaytline, Kaytlyn**

This name occurs in a variety of variants, as well as the abbreviated forms Cait, Cayt, Cass and Cassie. It is probable that all of these and the variants that are formed around Caitriona are borrowed via Latin from Greek *Aikaterinë*, the name of a young woman martyred in Alexandria in the early years of the fourth century. St Catherine's name came to be associated with courage and purity, qualities that were attractive to the Celts. One of the most beautiful stories associated with the Irish form of the name relates to the Countess Cathleen who, during a time of famine, offered her soul to the devil in exchange for food for the starving. When she died, the devil came to collect her soul but God refused to allow him to keep it, saying that Cathleen deserved to go straight to heaven because she was willing to

give up not just her life but her salvation for others.

SEE: **Katell**

Caitríona, Catriona (pronounced to rhyme with 'cat + tree + on + a')

Caitríona is popular in Ireland, Scotland and the Isle of Man. Like Kathleen, it may be a borrowing from Greek *Aikaterinë* and is thought to mean 'clear, pure'. The form Catriona was popularised by Robert Louis Stevenson's sequel to *Kidnapped*, which was called *David Balfour* in America and *Catriona* in Britain.

Camryn

The spelling looks Welsh but this name is often a female form of *cam shrón* (meaning 'crooked nose'!), Cameron.

SEE: **Cameron**

Caoilfhinn (pronounced like 'kay + lin'), **Kaylin, Kaylynn, Keelan, Keelin**

Caoilfhinn comes directly from *caoil fhinn*, meaning 'slender and fair' and implying 'very beautiful'.

SEE: **Keelan**

Cara, Caragh (pronounced like 'car + in')

Cara is the Irish word for 'friend'. It is possible that it was originally borrowed from Latin. Indeed, *cara* in Italian still means 'beloved'.

Carol, Caryl, Caryll, Carys

The name Carol is often a form of Latin *Carolus*, meaning 'Charles', reinforced by the word 'carol' meaning a Christmas hymn. However, the Irish name *Cearbhall* or *Cearúl*, probably meaning 'courageous in war', was anglicised as Car(r)ol(l) and so may have contributed to the popularity of the name. The Welsh *cariad*, meaning 'beloved', has helped to popularise Caryl and Carys in Wales.

Caronwyn (pronounced like 'car + on + in')

This Welsh name comes from car + *gwyn* and means 'love + fair', implying 'beautiful loved one'. It is possible that it was influenced by French *Cheron*, occasionally *Caron*, also meaning 'beloved, dear one'.

Cathbodua (pronounced like 'cah + bo + dwa')

Cathbodua was a Celtic war goddess and her name may come from *cath-bhuadhach*, meaning 'victorious in war', although it is sometimes said to mean 'raven of war'. *Badhbh*, means 'scald crow', which feeds on corpses and *cathbhadhbh* means 'battle-scald crow'! In all Celtic communities, there is a tradition that crows, ravens and rooks foretell sudden or violent death.

Cathleen, Cathline
SEE: **Caitlín**

Ceara
SEE: **Caera, Ciara**

Ceasg (pronounced like 'cask')

Ceasg may come from *ceasach*, meaning 'dark, sorrowful'. The name can be used as an individual name or as the generic name for a Scottish mermaid who has the body of a beautiful woman and the golden tail of a salmon. Like many Celtic supernatural beings, if Ceasg is caught, she can give her captor three wishes. She can also marry a human man and bear his children – all of whom will have webbed toes – but she will eventually return to the sea. Matthew Arnold reversed this story in his poem 'The Forsaken Merman' when a human woman lived with a merman and bore his children but eventually went back to the land and:

> She left lonely for ever
> The kings of the sea.

Ceinlys (pronounced like 'cane + liss')

This Welsh name may be a blend of *tlws*, 'gems' + *melys*, 'sweet', and so imply beauty, wealth and sweetness of character.

Ceiridwen, Ceridwen (pronounced like 'care + id + win')

This Welsh name is probably a blend of *cerdd*, 'poetry' + *gwen*, 'pure, fair, white'. An early Ceridwen was the goddess of poetry and was married to Tegid Foel. One legend about Ceridwen tells how she pursued a young man who had inadvertently stolen some of her wisdom. To avoid her, he was transformed into a grain of corn, but she changed herself into a chicken and swallowed him. Nine months later, she gave birth to Taliesin, who was thought to be the greatest poet of the Celtic world.

Ceri, Cerian, Kerry (pronounced like County Kerry)

Ceri is popular in Wales and Cornwall and is sometimes used as a spelling for Kerry. It is not certain whether it is a shortened form of Ceridwen, meaning 'beautiful as a poem' or whether it is Welsh *car*, which is the equivalent of Irish *cara*. The Welsh verb *caru* means 'to love'.

Cessair (pronounced like 'kess + air')

The *Lebor Gabala* or Book of Invasions tells the story of how Cessair arrived in Ireland with fifty-three women and three men. When her husband died, she could not be consoled and died shortly after him. The elements were so saddened that it rained and rained until all of Ireland was covered with water. It is not certain what Cessair's name means but it may be from *ceas*, 'coracle', or its homophone *ceas*, meaning 'sorrow, affliction'.

Chevonne
SEE: **Siobhán**

Ciara, Ciarra, Keera, Keira, Keyra, Kiera, Kira, Kyara (all pronounced like 'key're + a')

Ciara is a feminine form of Ciaran and comes from *ciar*, meaning 'dark, dark brown'. Like its male equivalent, it can be spelt in a variety of ways, including all of the above.

Cigfa (pronounced like 'kig + fa')

Cigfa's name may be related to Welsh *cigfran*, 'raven'. Cigfa was married to Pryderi, the king of Dyfed, who was abducted from this world when he found a golden bowl and got stuck to it. Cigfa lived with her father-in-law until he was able to rescue Pryderi.

Clarisant (pronounced like 'klar + ees + ant'), Clarisse

The name seems to be of French origin, related to *clair*, *clarisse*, meaning 'light, clear'. Clarisant or possibly Clarisse or Clarissa was the sister of Gawain, a Knight of the Round Table. Her mother was Morgause, a Cornish princess who married the Lord of Orkney.

Clíodhna, Cleona (pronounced like 'klee + en + a')

Clíodhna or Clíona is sometimes also spelt Cleona. Its meaning is uncertain, although it may be related to *clódhna*, 'exceptionally thin' or *cliath*, the word for a system of musical notation, and this would be appropriate as Clíodhna is sometimes described as a poetic muse. In some legends, Clíodhna loses her beloved and cannot find rest without him; in others, she has many young lovers.

Clodagh (pronounced like 'clo + da')

It seems likely that Clodagh or Clóda

has been taken over from the *Clóideach*, the name of a river in Tipperary. In this it resembles Shannon. Clodagh is also sometimes used as the Irish equivalent of Claudia, a Latin nickname originally meaning 'lame'.

Codi, Cody, Kodi, Kody

This name is the result of dropping the 'Ma' from Mac Óda, 'son of the prosperous one', so that the surname became Coda or Cody. It means 'prosperity, fortune' and is more frequently used as the name of a boy than a girl. However, the popularity of Cody Willis in the Australian soap *Neighbours* has resulted in a number of female Codies, spelt in a variety of ways.

Coinchend (pronounced like 'ko + in + hend')

The meaning of this name may be related to *coingheall*, 'covenant, pledge'. According to tradition, Coinchend was a queen who tried to prevent her daughter getting married because of a prophecy that she would die as soon as her daughter found a husband. Such legends are reminiscent of the myths that describe the new year as a baby and the old year as a dying old man. As in all such stories, Coinchend is doomed to failure, even though she hides her daughter in a fortress.

Colleen

The name Colleen or Colene or Coleen comes from the Gaelic word *cailín*, meaning 'girl'. It was used by people of Irish descent in America, Australia and South Africa and was popularised by the Australian novelist Colleen McCullough, whose televised novel *The Thorn Birds* attracted a large audience in Britain.

Columba, Koulm, Koulmia

As well as the Irish male saint Columba, there was a fourth-century Cornish female saint of the same name, coming from Latin *columba*, meaning 'dove'. The stories about the Cornish Columba are confused. It seems that her parents were Lodan and Maingild and they wanted her to marry a pagan prince of noble birth. Columba refused and was martyred. According to different accounts, she was martyred in Brittany, or France or Germany. It is even possible that she was one of the virgins martyred with St Ursula or that, indeed, there were several female saints of this name. The related names Koulm and Koulmia are still used in Brittany.

Cora, Coralie

The name Cora and the French Coralie both seem to derive from a Greek word *korë*, meaning 'maiden'. In this sense, they parallel Colleen. The name Cora and occasionally Córa are, however, used in parts of Ireland as a feminine form of Corey, which is a common surname.

SEE: **Corey**

Cordelia

Many people argue, plausibly, that

Cordelia comes from Latin *cor*, meaning 'heart', blended with Delia, from the Greek placename, *Delos*. However, Shakespeare drew his story of *King Lear* from Celtic sources and there are Celtic equivalents for Lear, Regan and Goneril. It is possible that Cordelia, then, is a Celtic name coming from such a noun as *cóiridheacht*, meaning 'propriety' or *córdadh*, 'equality, harmony'.

Corey, Cori, Kori

These names may be versions of Cora, from Greek *korë*, 'maiden' they may come from the Irish surname Corey, which is probably a form of the Germanic name Godfrey, from *god* + *frid*, meaning 'the peace of God'.

Creiddylad (pronounced like 'cred + dil + lad')

Creiddylad is another example of a strong-willed Celt. It is not certain what her name means, although it may be associated with the Welsh *creyr*, 'heron'. She was the daughter of Lud or Llud who is said to have named Trinovantum after himself as *Caer Llud(ein)*, 'the Fort of Lud', or London.

Creidne (pronounced like 'credge + nih')

Creidne was a warrior and her name probably comes from *creidiún*, 'honour, faith'. Female warriors were part of the Celtic tradition and Creidne was a member of the Fianna, an Irish equivalent of Arthur's Knights of the Round Table. The Fianna, or warriors of destiny, had many leaders, the best known of whom is Fionn MacCool. In order to be accepted into the Fianna, a warrior like Creidne would have had to pass several initiation tests. She would have to have been a good athlete, skilled in arms, courageous enough to stand still while spears were thrown at her, and she would also have to have been a fine poet. It is perhaps worth stressing that women and men both wrote poetry in the various Celtic languages.

Creirwy (pronounced like 'crer + we')

Creirwy, whose name may come from *creyr* + *gwyn* and mean 'fair crane', was renowned as one of the most beautiful maidens in the Welsh tradition.

Crisiant (pronounced like 'kris + ee + ent')

This name probably comes from Welsh *crisial*, meaning 'crystal'.
SEE: **Crystal**

Cruatha (pronounced like 'crew + a + ha')

Cruatha was the mother of Queen Maeve, whose story is recorded in *Táin Bó Cualigne* (The Cooley Cattle-Raid). Her name may carry the meaning of 'firm, solid'.

Crystal, Kristell, Krystell

Crystal is an example of the popularity of gemstones as the name for a girl. This one comes from Greek

C

krystallos, 'ice', but it has been reinforced in Celtic communities by the existence of the surname 'McCrystal', by the Celtic words for 'Christian', and by the medieval legend of Crystabel(l). She is an interesting character in that she has a series of adventures, including becoming betrothed to her own son. Unlike the Greek tragedy of Oedipus and Jocasta, Crystabell discovered the problem before the marriage was consummated. The name Krystell is found in Brittany and this form of the name is likely to become more popular.

Cyhyreath (pronounced like 'koo + hoo + reeth')

Cyhyreath's name may mean 'weeping, lamentation'. Cyhyreath is a Welsh equivalent of the Irish banshee or a Scottish *caoineag*, whose visit to a house foretells a death.

D

Dacey, Dacie

Although the link is not immediately apparent, this name is related to Desmond in that they both involve the use of Gaelic *deas*, meaning 'south', so Dacey means 'southern girl'.
SEE: **Desmond**

Daimhín, Davina (pronounced like 'daw + veen')

These names are thought to be from the same source but they seem to have arisen separately in Ireland and Scotland. *Daimhín* means 'little deer' and it has produced the surnames Davane and Devine (although the Northern Ireland Devines often claim that they are descended from the Spanish Da Vinas). Davina is used in Scotland as a feminine form of David, but the Celtic influence from *daimhín* may have contributed to its popularity.

Dáiligh, Daley, Daly

This is usually a surname in Ireland but, like Kelly, it has been used as a given name. It is probably related to *dáil*, 'meeting', or *dálach*, 'attender of meetings', and so could be a useful omen for the dynamic business woman of the 21st century!

Daireann, Darran, Darina (pronounced like 'dar + rawn')

Daireann probably comes from *dáir* and means 'fruitful, bountiful', although it may also be related to *dair*, 'oak tree'. One of the earliest references we have to Daireann is to a beautiful young woman who fell in love with Fionn MacCool and wanted him as her husband – for a year.
SEE: **Darfhinn**

Daley, Daly
SEE: **Dáiligh**

Damhnaid (pronounced like 'dav + nidge'), **Damhnait** (pronounced like 'dhow + nid')
SEE: **Dymphna**

Dana, Danu, Dayna

This is one of the oldest names in the Celtic tradition. *Dana* or *Danu* or *Anu* seems to have been a mother god, revered in Indo-European traditions from India to Ireland. It is not certain what her name means but it is associated with power and generosity. In Ireland, it is further reinforced by the Gaelic words *dán*, meaning 'poem', and *dána*, meaning 'brave, daring'. The name was popular in the United States because of the male star, Dana Andrews, whose name probably meant 'a Dane'. The first syllable may rhyme with 'ran' or with 'rain'.

SEE: **Don**

Dara, Deri

Dara is a Gaelic name coming from *dair* meaning 'oak' and is related to the word *doire*, meaning 'oak grove', from which Derry is derived. The name may be either male or female but there is a tendency for Dara and Deri to refer to girls and Darach and Derry to be preserved for boys.

SEE: **Darach**

Darcy, D'Arcy, Darsey

It seems likely that the name 'D'Arcy' was taken to Ireland by the Normans, because the name has a long history in France and a meaning associated with 'fortress'. In Ireland, the name was reinforced by a Gaelic adjective *dorcha* meaning 'dark, dark-haired'. Darcy is appropriate therefore for a dark-haired child.

Darfhinn (pronounced like 'dar + rin'), Dairinn, Dareena, Darena, Darina, Daron

This name may well be a modified form of Dara with the diminutive ending *-ín*. There was an Irish princess with this name who was married to the king of Leinster. The modern spelling has probably been influenced by Doreen, which means 'gift'. There is also the name Darfhinn or Dairinn, which seems to mean 'daughter of Finn' or possibly 'golden-haired daughter', where 'finn' is the adjective 'fair'.

Dearbhail, Dearbhal (pronounced like 'jar + ville'), Deirbhile (pronounced like 'jar + villa' or 'jer + villa'), Dervla

The name Dearbhail seems to be related to *dearbha*, meaning 'genuineness' and Deirbhile may be *deirbh + file*, meaning 'daughter or relative of the poet', but they have both contributed to Dervla, and so are treated under the same heading. Dervla Murphy, the writer, has popularised the name even in Cameroon in West Africa among people who have enjoyed reading *Cameroon with Egbert*.

Dearbhorgaill, Devorgilla (pronounced like 'der + vor + gill + a')

This name may be a development from Dearbhail or it may be *deirbh + Forgall* and mean 'daughter or relative of Forgall'. There are two Devorgillas, at least, in Irish literary tradition. The first was in love with Cúchulainn and was angry when he rejected her. However, they settled their differences and became as close as brother and sister. The second was a twelfth-century queen who ran away from her husband to live with Diarmuid, the man she loved.

Dechtire (pronounced like 'deck + tir + ra')

Dechtire was the sister of Conchubhar and the mother of Cúchulainn. Her name may be related to the number *deich*, 'ten', possibly suggesting 'tenth child'. Her legend suggests that she was seized by the Sidhe, or supernatural beings, and transformed into a bird. For part of the time, she regained her feminine form, and on one of these occasions she slept with Lugh who was, thus, the father of Cúchulainn.

Dee

Dee may come from a Welsh adjective *du*, meaning 'black' and thus be appropriate for a dark-haired child. It could also derive from the River Dee and can be used as an abbreviation for any name beginning with 'D'.

Deirdre (pronounced like 'dear + dree' or 'dare + drih'), Deirdriú, Deidre

The meaning of Deirdre is not certain although it may be related to *deireadh*, meaning 'end'. Her love story is one of the most beautiful in Celtic literature. She was betrothed to King Conchubhar but was in love with Naoise, one of the sons of Usna. Deirdre and Naoise ran away to Scotland with Naoise's brothers. They were tricked into returning to Ireland where Naoise was killed. Deirdre threw herself from a chariot rather than live without the man she loved.

Delbchaem, Delebchaim (pronounced like 'del + eb + hime')

According to Welsh traditions, Delbchaem was the daughter of King Morgan and Queen Coinchend. Her name probably includes the adjective *del*, meaning 'pretty'. She was kept apart from people because a prophecy suggested that Coinchend would die if her daughter ever married. Only Art managed to overcome all the obstacles put between him and the beautiful Delbchaem.

Delia
SEE: Dilic

Delwyn, Delwin (pronounced like 'del + win')

There are many Welsh names beginning with Del-, all of them related to *del* implying 'pretty'. Delwyn suggests both 'pretty' and 'fair'.

Demelza (pronounced like 'dem + el + za')

Demelza is a Cornish placename that has become popular for girls especially since the television series *Poldark*, in which the heroine was Demelza. The meaning is unclear, although it may be related to the Cornish word for 'parable' and the form has possibly been influenced by the French *demoiselle*, 'young girl'.

Derryth (pronounced like 'der + rith'), **Derry, Deri**
This particular name is Welsh and is related to *derw*, 'oaken', and *derwydd*, 'druid'. The name is close in form and meaning to Gaelic *doire*, meaning 'oak grove'.
SEE: **Dara**

Devin, Devon
Both these names have been inspired by the English county, whose Celtic name seems to mean 'deep valley'. They could also have been influenced by Welsh *dewin*, 'magician', and Gaelic *dán*, 'gift'.

Devorgilla
SEE: **Dearbhorgaill**

Dilic, Dilecq, Dilecta, Dilie, Dillie, Dilys (pronounced like 'dill + iss')
Forms of this name occur in Brittany, Cornwall, Ireland and Wales, and they may have nothing in common but their similarity of form. It is possible that there were two Cornish saints, one Dilic and one Dilie or that, indeed, neither really existed, although there are references to both these forms in lists of early saints. The form Dilecq seems to have been used in Brittany as well as the latinised form Dilecta, which has the implication of 'beloved'. Dilie and

Dillie occurred in Ireland as forms of Delia, a Greek name meaning 'from Delos', and this usage may have been reinforced by the Irish adjective *dílis*, 'genuine, proper'. Welsh Dilys seems to have come from the adjective *dilys*, 'genuine'.

Dimpna
SEE: **Dymphna**

Dindrane (pronounced like 'din + drain')
Dindrane was the sister of Perceval, a Knight of the Round Table. The meaning of her name is uncertain, although it may be linked to the Welsh adjective *dinam*, 'immaculate'. Dindrane is an icon of beauty, courtesy and true generosity. According to legend, she met a leper who could only be saved by receiving her blood. Dindrane gave her blood willingly and the leper woman was cured.

Dogmaela (pronounced like 'dog + mail + a')
Dogmaela is the female form of Dogmael, a name that seems to be related to Welsh *dogni*, 'apportion'. St Dogmael was a saint who had churches named after him in Brittany, Cornwall and Wales. The name continues to be used in Brittany in the forms Dogmaela and Dogmeela.
SEE: **Dogmael**

Dominica, Domhnacha (pronounced like 'doe + na + ha')
Dominica is, of course, a modification

of Latin *dominus*, meaning 'lord'. It was used in early Christian times to indicate that a girl was dedicated to God and it gained a second wave of popularity during the lifetime of St Dominic (1170-1221), the founder of the Dominican Order. There was a church dedicated to *Sancta Dominica* in south-east Cornwall in 1263 and she was reputed to be the daughter of an Irish king. The form Domhnacha may derive from Irish *Domhnach*, 'the Lord's Day', or from the same source as the surname Donaghy meaning 'brown-haired warrior'.

SEE: **Duncan**

Don

Don was the oldest Welsh mother god and is, therefore, in some ways, equivalent to Irish Dana. She is associated with water and her name is found in such rivers as the Danube in Europe and the Don in Yorkshire. She was thought to have taken up her home in the skies and the constellation Cassiopeia was called *Llys Don*, 'Don's Court'.

SEE: **Dana**

Donalda

Donalda is the female form of Scottish Donald, which comes from Scots Gaelic *Domhnul* and means 'ruler of the world'.

SEE: **Domhnal(l), Donal, Donald**

Donwenna (pronounced like 'don + wen + a')

SEE: **Dwyn**

Dorian, Dorien

Oscar Wilde seems to have created the name Dorian for the title character in *The Portrait of Dorian Gray*. This Dorian was a beautiful young man who led a dissolute life but retained his beautiful appearance. The marks of his dissipation were transferred to the portrait he kept in his attic. The name has been transferred to girls partly because of its similarity to Dora, Doreen and Doris, but Wilde may also have been influenced by the Irish name Dairinn, which meant 'daughter of Fionn MacCool'.

Drusa, Drusilla

The history of this name goes back over two thousand years and may be related to Druid or Gaelic *draoicheach*, 'magic'. It seems as if Drusus was a Gaulish name that was adopted by a Roman Livius who killed the Gaul, Drusus, in single combat. There is a reference to a St Drusa in Cornwall who seems to have made a pilgrimage to Rome in the fifth century. The name Drusilla is derived from Latin Drusus and is thus ultimately of Celtic origin.

Duana (pronounced like 'doo + awn + ah'), **Dwana**

Duana means 'dark little one' and comes from the Gaelic name *dubhán*, 'dark' or 'black', which is also anglicised as Duffin.

SEE: **Duane**

Dubh (pronounced like 'dhoo' or 'dhoov')

The word *dubh* or *du* means 'black, dark' in most of the Celtic languages. The Druid woman who gave her name to Dublin was called Dubh, and legend has it that she was cast into a pool by her husband because she killed his second wife. The name Dublin means 'black' + 'pool' or 'Dubh's pool', a name that the Romans translated as 'Nigratherma'.

Dubh Lacha (pronounced like 'do + loch + a')

Dubh Lacha was the beautiful wife of the seventh-century king of Leinster called Mongan. Her name seems to mean 'black duck' although the same word *lacha* was used as a term to mean 'beautiful girl'. Dubh Lacha ran away with Brandubh, her lover, but Mongan used all his skills in both magic and poetry to win her back.

Dwyn (pronounced like 'dwin'), **Donwenna** (pronounced like 'don + wen + na'), **Dwynwen** (pronounced like 'dwin + win')

According to Welsh legend, Dwyn or, less often, Donwenna or Dwynwen, was a princess and is the patron saint of lovers, even though she became a nun. Her name seems to be associated with 'holy' and 'fair'. Maelon wanted to marry her and she turned him into a block of ice. However, she relented and prayed that he might be restored, that all lovers might find fulfilment, and that

she might have the ultimate joy of never having to get married.

Dymphna, Dimpna (pronounced like 'dimf + na'), **Dympna, Damhnaid** (pronounced like 'dav + nid'), **Damhnait** (pronounced like 'dow + nid')

It is possible that Dymphna and Damhnaid are two different Irish names, both of which are related to *dán*, 'poetry'. St Dymphna was the seventh-century daughter of an Irish king. According to the legend, she fled to Belgium in order to become a nun. She is buried near Antwerp in Belgium.

Eachna (pronounced like 'ah + na' or 'ack + na')

This name seems to be derived from Gaelic *each*, meaning 'horse', and was possibly an Irish name for the goddess who was worshipped in Europe as Epona. Eachna was re-nowned for both her intelligence and her beauty.

SEE: **Epona**

Ealga (pronounced like 'al + ga')

Ealga means 'noble, brave'. It is sometimes used as a poetic name for Ireland, which is seen as female and represented by many female names including Caitlin, Erin, Roisin and, best known perhaps, Rosaleen, as in James Clarence Mangan's poem, 'Dark Rosaleen'.

Eamair, Eimear, Emer (pronounced like 'aim + er' or 'eem + er')
Cúchulainn's wife's name is most frequently represented as Emer although it is occasionally found as Eamhair in Scotland and pronounced like 'ayve + er'. It is not certain what the name means although it may be related to *eamhean*, 'twin'. Emer and Cúchulainn were betrothed when he was only seven but, although their marriage was arranged, they loved each other deeply. Cúchulainn was unfaithful to Emer many times but she found it easy to forgive him until she was replaced in his affections by Fand. When Cúchulainn died, Emer spoke movingly at his graveside before she too died. Like many of the great lovers of Ireland, they shared the same grave.

Eavan, Aoibhinn
Eavan is an anglicisation of *aoibhinn*, meaning 'attractive, beautiful, radiant'.

Edana, Edna
Edana and Edna are almost certainly anglicised forms of Eithne, which comes from *eithne*, 'nut kernel', or *aodh*, meaning 'fire'. The same name has been used for the mother of Sarah in the Apochryphal book of Tobit, but the Hebrew Edna derives from Eden, as in the Garden of Eden, and means 'pleasure' or 'perfect happiness'.
SEE: **Eithna**

Éibhleann, Eibhlín (pronounced like 'ayve + linn' or 'eve + linn'), **Eileen, Elaine**

Éibhleann is a Gaelic word, related to *aoibhinn*, meaning 'radiance' and it probably combined with biblical Eve, meaning 'life', and Norman Aveline and Elaine, 'like the sun', to provide all of the above names and their derivatives. The names continue to be popular in the Celtic areas as well as in many other parts of the world.
SEE: **Aibhlínn**

Eileen
The name Eileen is closely associated with Ireland and has featured in songs, poetry, and plays such as 'Eileen McManus' or 'Eileen a Rún', often symbolising the young woman who had to emigrate to help support her family:

> One day as I strolled along Broadway,
> A vision came into my view,
> A vision of sadness and beauty,
> A beauty that's given to few.
> There was I in the land of the stranger,
> There was she I'd not seen her before,
> But somehow I knew she was Irish,
> Sweet Eileen from Erin's green shore.
>
> (J.M. Crofts, 'Eileen McManus')

Éilis, Eibhlís (pronounced like 'eye + lish' or 'ail + ish')
These names were probably borrowed into Irish from Norman Alice, meaning 'noble', and reinforced by the Hebrew Elizabeth, meaning 'God

is my oath'. Many Irish names still have two or more pronunciations reflecting taste as well as regional differences.

SEE: **Aibhlis, Ailis**

Eilwen (pronounced like 'al + win')
Eilwen is from Welsh *œl* + *gwyn*, meaning 'fair brow', a phrase that is equivalent to 'beautiful'.

Eimear, Emer
SEE: **Eamair**

Einín, Eneen (pronounced like 'ain + een')
This name is from *éan* + *ín*, meaning 'little bird'. It is a recent coinage but is already popular. In Ireland, as elsewhere, endearments often took the form of birds. We find the practice in the English use of 'duck' in parts of England, 'hen' in parts of Scotland.

Éire (pronounced like 'air + rih')
Éire was a goddess who lived with her sisters Banba and Fódla in Ireland. Each of the three sisters wanted the country to be called after her and so they held a race. By a mixture of talent and guile, Éire won. In due course, the country became Éire and later Éire + land or Ireland.

Eireen (pronounced like 'i + reen'), **Éireann** (pronounced like 'air + in'), **Erin**
Eireen is possibly a blend of Irene, from Greek *eirene*, meaning 'peace', and Erin, meaning 'Ireland'. Éireann

is either a variant of Erin or a blend of Eire and Ann.
SEE: **Erin**

Eirwen
If Snow White had been given a Welsh name, she would have been called Eirwen, because *eira* means 'snow' and *gwyn* is 'white' or 'fair'.

Eithna (pronounced like 'eth + na')
Eithne, Ena, Enya, Ethniu
These names may all come from *eithne*, 'nut kernel', or be related to Aodh or Aidan and thus mean 'fire, little fire'. Eithne was a goddess who, like many of the early Celtic saints, refused to eat food but was sustained by drinking milk. There are several saints called Eithne and the name is currently experiencing a revival. It is possible that the name is a modification of Eachna, who was reputed to be the wisest and also the most beautiful woman in the world.
SEE: **Eachna, Edna, Endelient**

Elen
Elen is a Welsh form of Helen, which comes from Greek *helios*, 'sun' and means 'like the sun, sunbeam, radiant'. According to legend, Elen was extraordinarily beautiful. One night, a young warrior, Maxen, saw her in a dream and knew that his life would never be complete until Elen was his wife.

Elspeth
Elspeth is a Scottish form of Elizabeth, which is a Hebrew name

meaning 'God is my oath'.
SEE: **Iseabeal**

Eluned (pronounced like 'ell + in + ed')
Eluned is a Welsh name probably from *eilun*, meaning 'image, object of adoration'. Like many traditional Welsh names, it is being revived and used again for daughters.

Elwa, Elwy
These names come from Welsh *elwa*, meaning 'profit, benefit'.

Emer
SEE: **Eamair**

Ena
Ena is sometimes regarded as a pet form of Eithne and so means 'little fire'. It has also been used as an abbreviation for Eugenia, from Greek *eugenios*, meaning 'nobly born'.

Enat, Aodhnaid, Aodhnait
(pronounced like 'ey + net')
Enat, is a female form of Aidan and means 'little fire'. The name is similar in form to Welsh *enaid*, meaning 'soul', and may have been reinforced by the Gaelic *ionailt*, meaning 'handmaid'. For many Celtic monks and nuns, the idea of being a servant or a handmaid of a saint was extremely attractive and there are hundreds of stories of how young religious 'apprenticed' themselves to saints.

Enda, Eneda
Enda derives from Gaelic *éan*, meaning 'bird', and suggests freedom of spirit. In the Gospels, the Holy Ghost was seen as a dove, and in Irish tradition, the soul going to heaven is represented as a bird. The sixth-century St Enda was a monk and the name has traditionally been given to boys but, because the 'a' ending is used widely in Europe for girls' names, Enda is occasionally given to girls. This tendency is reinforced by the fact that there is a Cornish female saint called Eneda.

Endelient (pronounced like 'en + dell + ee + ent')
Endelient is a Cornish saint and seems to have been one of the twenty-four children of St Brechanus and his wife Gladys or Gladuse. Like many of the early Celtic saints, she lived a life of great simplicity and austerity: she is reputed to have given up all food and to have drunk only milk and water. Her name may be related to Eithne and Enid and may thus mean 'fire', 'soul' or 'life'. According to legend, her cow frequently strayed onto a farmer's land and one day, in anger, he killed it. When King Arthur heard what had happened, he had the farmer executed. Endelient, however, prayed ceaselessly and both the farmer and her cow were miraculously brought back to life.
SEE: **Eithna**

Endellion
Endellion is, almost certainly, another form of Endelient, which is

related to Irish *aodh*, 'fire' and Welsh *enaid*, 'soul' and thus may mean 'fire, soul'. Her miracles were so highly regarded that, before she died, there were rows as to where her body should be buried. St Endellion ordered that, on her death, her body should be placed on a cart that was drawn by two oxen and that the burial should take place at the spot where the oxen stopped.

Eneen
SEE: **Einín**

Enid, Enida
Enid probably comes from Welsh *enaid*, meaning 'soul' and suggesting 'purity of soul'. One of the Enids in Celtic literature was the wife of Geraint ap Erbin and she was unhappy because her husband thought more highly of comfortable living than of fighting on the battlefield. When Geraint asked her why she was depressed, she refused to answer and he thought she must have a lover. To prevent her seeing this lover, Geraint took Enid with him when he went off to battle. Eventually, Geraint realised that Enid loved only him, and Enid learned to appreciate home comforts.

Enora
Enora is a Breton form of Latin *honoria*, meaning 'honour'. The pronunciation is influenced by French *Honore*, where the 'h' is not sounded.
SEE: **Nora**

Enya
Enya may come from *eithne*, 'nut kernel', or may mean 'flame'. The name may have started as a form of Eithne or Áine, meaning 'brightness', but the popularity of the Donegal musician has ensured that Enya is now being treated as a name in its own right.
SEE: **Eithna, Áine**

Epona
Epona was a goddess whose name may be related to Welsh *epil*, 'breed'. She was probably originally Celtic but was honoured by the Romans. She was renowned as a horserider and was reputed to carry warriors who died bravely in battle straight to paradise. Epona, like Macha, gave birth to twin boys who were destined to be heroes.
SEE: **Eachna, Macha**

Erin, Erina, Eriu
Erin is a modified form of Éire the goddess after whom Ireland was named. Her name sometimes appears as Ériu or Ériu. She was a member of the *Tuatha de Danaan*, 'the people of Dana' or the ancient gods of Ireland. The form Erina suggests 'Irish girl' and has been influenced in form by Erena, meaning 'peace'.
SEE: **Eireen**

Ertha, Eartha
The name Eartha is probably most closely associated with the American singer, Eartha Kitt, but St Ertha's name is recorded in Cornwall. The

name may be related to *arddeliad*, meaning 'strong faith, firm belief'.

Erwanez

This is a Breton name, the female equivalent of Erwan, which may be related to Irish Éireamhóin, Scottish Irvine or Welsh Erwan.

SEE: **Éireamhóin**

Essylt

This name is similar to the Irish Yseult but is from Welsh and means 'exceptionally beautiful'.

Etain, Étáin (pronounced like 'ey + taw + in' or 'ee + taw + in'), Eadain

Etain's name occurs in several forms including Édáin and the Gaelic *Éadaoin*. Her name may play on the Gaelic word *éad*, meaning 'jealousy'. Etain became Midhir's second wife, but when his first wife, Fuamnach, found out, she transformed Etain into a fly that was blown about by the wind for seven years. Eventually, the fly fell into a glass of wine that was drunk by a woman who longed for a child. Nine months later, she gave birth to a beautiful daughter who was called Etain, and this Etain married Eochaidh, the High King.

Ethna, Ethne, Ethniú

These names may all come from *eithne*, 'nut kernel' or from *aodh*, 'fire'. Many traditional Irish stories involve the milk from magical cows. According to tradition, Ethna or Eithne lived on milk alone as a means

of purifying her body. A similar story is told about Endellion and Endelient, so it is possible that these names are Cornish variants of Eithne or Ethniu.

SEE: **Eithne**

Eulalia

Eulalia was one of three sisters. Eulalia, Serena and Sapientia went on a pilgrimage with St Ursula and they were all martyred on the way home to Cornwall. Eulalia is Greek in origin and means 'fair of speech'; the others are Latin and mean 'serene' and 'wisdom'. The Celtic forms of the name are not recorded but, since they were used in a Celtic area over 1,600 years ago, they seem to qualify as Celtic names!

Eurielle

Eurielle is not as common in English-speaking regions as it once was. It means 'angelic' and may have been influenced by Hebrew *Uriel*, which means 'God is my light'.

Eurwen

This Welsh name combines *aur*, 'gold' and *gwyn* 'fair' and may thus be taken as the equivalent of 'beautiful, golden girl'.

Fachanan ((pro nounced 'fokt + na'), Fachnan, Fachtna (pronounced like 'fah + a + nan' or 'foh + a + nan')

Fachanan probably comes from *fach*,

'challenge', and may mean 'hostile', a name that was appropriate for a person who was hostile to sin. It can be given to either a girl or a boy. The sixth-century Fachanan was devoted to scholarship.

Fainche (pronounced like 'fan + che' or 'fan + ke' or 'fine + che')
Although this Irish name looks remarkably similar to the Breton form of Francis, it is unrelated and occurs in a variety of related spellings, including Faenche and Fanchea. It is not clear what the name means but it may be related to *faing*, 'raven', or *fáineóir*, 'wanderer'. One of the saints to bear this name was the sister of Enda.

Fáinne (pronounced like 'faw + in + nye')
This is the Irish word *fáinne*, meaning 'ring' and also 'halo'. It is not a traditional name but it has been used because it is both attractive and unusual.

Fallon

This name is more usual as the surnames Fallon and Falloon, from *fallamhan*, meaning 'leader'. It is attractive, however, and has become popular in America, possibly because of the influence of one of the characters in the soap opera, *Dynasty*.

Fanch, Franseza, Soaz

Fanch is the Breton equivalent of Francis and the name is occasionally used for a girl, although the forms Franseza and Soaz are preferred. Like all forms of Francis, Fanch means 'from France' and it was originally a nickname. The most popular St Francis was probably St Francis of Assisi, whose attitude to animals and plants was strictly 'green'. He was called John but came to be known as Francis because of his family's business links with France.

Fand

Fand was the wife of Manannan, the god of the sea. We do not know exactly what her name meant although it may be related to *fán*, 'stray'. Fand loved Cúchulainn who, for a time, returned her passion. When he left her, she returned to Manannan and he kindly shook his cloak between Fand and Cúchulainn so that they would never meet again.

Fay

This name may have originated in France, where *foi* used to be pronounced like 'fway' and meant 'faith'. It was, however, absorbed into Irish culture where a person may still be described as 'fay', meaning 'having mystical powers' or 'fated'. It is thought by some to be a short form of Faith and is thus linked to 'fidelity'.

Fedelma, Fidelma

This traditional Gaelic name goes back at least 1,500 years and has been held by saint and warrior. Its Celtic meaning is not certain although it may be linked to *feidhle*, meaning 'constancy'. It closely resembles Latin names, such as Fidelia, which has the attractive meaning of 'the faithful one'.

Feenat, Fianat, Fiadhnaid, Fiadhnait (pronounced like 'fee + en + et', 'fe + en + id')

This Gaelic name comes from *fian*, 'wild thing', and means 'small deer'. It is in the Celtic tradition of not drawing a sharp line between animals and humans. Many humans were transformed into animals and several animals, including the deer, the seal and the salmon, were known to have the ability, under certain circumstances, to change into humans.

Fenella

This name is a modern version of Gaelic Fionnuala, meaning 'fair shoulders' and implying 'very beautiful'. There is a partial pun in Gaelic with *fionnubhall*, literally 'white apple' but meaning 'grape'. The word *fion(n)*, as in Fiona, can mean 'wine'.

Ffion

Ffion is occasionally used in Wales and is usually a Welsh spelling of Fiona. Welsh uses 'ff-' for some borrowed words, such as *ffigur*, 'figure', and *ffiwsio*, 'to fuse'.
SEE: **Fiona**

Fflur

Fflur is a Welsh name, meaning 'flower' and roughly equivalent to Blodwyn. It seems to have been borrowed from French *Fleur*. Fflur was reputed to be so beautiful that lovers went on quests all over the known world in the hope of winning her.
SEE: **Blanaid, Blodwyn**

Fiadhnaid, Fiadhnait
SEE: **Feenat**

Fianat
SEE: **Feenat**

Fianna

The Fenian band of warriors was known as the Fianna and the name has begun to be given to girls, partly because it seems to be a blend of Fiona, 'wine', and Anna, 'full of grace'. Although Fionn's warriors were usually men, there is a strong tradition of Celtic women fighting side by side with men, a tradition described in Melvin Bragg's novel, *Credo*.

Fidelma
SEE: **Fedelma**

Finola
SEE: **Fionnuala**

Findabair (pronounced like 'finn + dab + air')

Findabair, whose name involves *fionn*, 'fair', and means 'fair portion' or *fionn* + *siabhár*, 'fair spectre', is in a long tradition of Celtic women who were fated to love only once. Findabair was the daughter of Maeve and Ailill and was in love with Fraoch. Fraoch, however, was incapable of paying her bride price but Maeve agreed to waive this if Fraoch fought on her behalf against Ulster's champion, Cúchulainn. Fraoch was killed and the loyal Findabair died of a broken heart.

Fiona, Ffiona

Fiona is extremely popular throughout the British Isles but is often associated with Scotland. It seems that Fiona has two possible sources. One is from Latin *vinum*, 'wine', which is *fíon* in modern Irish. The second is from *f(i)on(n)*, meaning 'fair, white, beautiful'.
SEE: **Ffion**

Fionnuala, Fionola, Finola, Fenella

One of the most beautiful stories in Celtic mythology centres on Fionnuala, whose name comes from *fionnghuala* and means 'fair shoulders'. According to legend, King Lír and his wife Aobh had a daughter, Fionnuala, and three sons, Aedh, Conn and Fiachra. When Aobh died, Lír's new wife, Aoife, was jealous of her husband's love for his children and bribed a sorcerer to kill them. The sorcerer could not take away the lives of such pure children and so transformed them into swans and condemned them to spend 300 years in the Moyle, the channel between Ireland and Scotland, 300 years in the Irish Sea and 300 years in the Atlantic.

Fírinne (pronounced like 'feer + ing + eh')

This name, which comes from *fírinne*, means 'truth, fidelity, genuineness', and is sometimes used as an attractive Irish equivalent of Verity.

Flaitheas (pronounced like 'flah + hish')

Flaitheas, meaning 'sovereignty' and implying also 'princely generosity', was the name of a goddess who judged Niall, the ancestor of the O'Neills, to be an acceptable chieftain. Generosity was not an option in Celtic tradition: it was an essential part of one's humanity. To be mean was to be less than human.

Flanna

Flanna is the female form of Flann and so means 'bright red'. Many people find it attractive because it includes Anna, a name that means 'full of grace'.

Fodla, Fodhla (pronounced like 'fo + la')

Fodla was a goddess, whose sisters were Banba and Eriú. Each of the sisters wanted Ireland to be called after her. It is not certain what her name means but it may be related to *fódúil*, meaning 'substantial'.
SEE: **Eriú**

Frann

Frann is an attractive name that suggests freedom and may come from *fraochán*, 'sea bird'.

Franseza

SEE: **Fanch**

Fuamnach (pronounced like 'foo + um + nach' or 'foo + um + knock')

Fuamnach was the wife of King Midhir and, like Queen Victoria, she was 'not amused' when her husband brought home a new wife, Etain. She felt she had no alternative but to take drastic action and so she changed her husband's favourite into a fly. It is not clear what her name means, although it may be related to Gaelic *fuaimneach*, meaning 'resounding'. It is certainly true that Etain's fate has resounded for the best part of two millennia.

Gael, Gaelle, Gail, Gayle

(pronounced like 'gale')

Gael, or *gaedheal*, is occasionally used in Celtic communities as the name of a Gaelic-speaker or a person who is from Ireland, Scotland or the Isle of Man. The selection of Gael as a girl's name has been influenced by the abbreviated form of Abigail, a Hebrew name that means 'Father of Exaltation'.

Ganeida

Ganeida was Merlin's sister. The name is a form of *Gwendydd*, and means 'morning star'.

Gaynor, Jenniver

Gaynor is probably an anglicised form of Guinevere, which comes from Welsh *gwyn*, 'white, pure' + *hwyfar*, 'smooth', and means 'fair and beautiful'. The name was, at one time,

so popular that it had a Cornish form, Jenniver, which has developed into a name in its own right.

SEE: Guinevere

Gearóidín (pronounced like 'gar + ro + dean')

Gearóidín is the Irish form of Geraldine and is quite widely used. It comes from Germanic *gar* + *wald*, 'spear' + 'rule' and means 'noble warrior' or 'spear carrier'. Although Gerald is Germanic, the name is appropriate because women were often warriors in Celtic communities.

Gethan, Gethen, Gethin

(pronounced like 'geth + an')

Gethan comes from a Welsh nickname *cethin*, meaning 'dark, swarthy'. It has been influenced in spelling by Bethan.

Gilda

Gilda is a Gaelic name from *giolla* + *Dia*, meaning 'servant of God'. 'Gil-' was often used in Irish and Scottish communities to mean people who devoted themselves to another, and so we get Gilchrist, 'the servant of Christ'. The term 'gilly' or 'gillie' is still used in Scottish English to mean 'an attendant' or 'a fishing and hunting guide'. The adjective *gile* means 'brightness, whiteness, the purest of the pure' and so the name could also mean 'the perfection of God'.

Gladys, Gladez, Gwladus, Gladuse (pronounced like 'glad + iss')

Gladys is an anglicised form of Welsh *Gwladys*, meaning 'delicate flower' or possibly being a Welsh form of Latin Claudia. The name was popular in Brittany, where it occurs as Gladez, and in Cornwall where St Gwladus(e) was a popular saint.

Glenda, Glenna

These Welsh variants probably come from Welsh *glan*, 'clean', + *da*, 'good' and imply 'purity' or they may be from *glyn*, 'valley' and mean 'girl from the valley'. The name has been popularised by Glenda Jackson, the actress who became a politician.

Glenys, Glynis, Glynys

(pronounced like 'glen + iss' or 'glin + iss')

Glenys may be a blend of Glenda and Gladys, or it may be a form of Glynis, from *glyn*, 'valley', and meaning 'valley girl'.

Gobhnet, Gobnaid (pronounced like 'gub + nidge'), Gobnait

(pronounced like 'gub + nit')

Gobnait's name is often given as the Irish equivalent of Barbara, which means 'foreign woman'. The fifth-century nun of this name built her chapel in Ballyvourney, on the spot where she saw nine white deer. It is also possible that the first part of the name comes from Irish *gob*, meaning 'mouth', and may have been applied to one who was skilled with words. Goibhniú, the Irish Vulcan, was god of the forge. His nickname was *'Gobán Saor'* and Gobnait was his goddess.

Gormflath (pronounced like 'gorom + la'), Gormla, Gormlaith (pronounced like 'gorom + lee')

Gormflath was an Irish queen, the wife of Brian Ború and the mother of the king of Dublin. She was partly Viking and was acknowledged to be a beauty. Her name is said to mean 'famed lady' but the first part may come from Gaelic *gorm* + *flaith*, 'blue' but also 'noble' + 'prince, chief'.

Gráinne, Grania (pronounced like 'graw + nya' or 'gra + in + nyih)

Gráinne's name may be derived from *gráidhte* and so mean 'the loved one', or it may mean 'grain of corn', thus linking her with an earlier goddess of the harvest. Her story is another example of the strength of purpose of traditional Irish heroines. She was the daughter of Cormac Mac Art and had been promised in marriage to the king, Fionn MacCool. When Gráinne saw him at the wedding feast, she knew he was too old for her. She fell in love instead with Fionn's nephew, Diarmuid, and she encouraged him to run away with her. Their punishment was a curse that prevented them spending two consecutive nights in the same place.

Granuaile (pronounced like 'gran + ye + wail')

Granuaile or Gráinne Ní Mháille (Grace O'Malley) was a sea captain who travelled the known trade routes until her death in 1603. She attacked

English ships and spent periods in jail for piracy. If someone had created a fictional character like Granuaile, critics would have said it was too far-fetched. She was a wife, a mother, a clan leader, a patriot and a renowned sailor. Her fame was celebrated in verse and song and she came to be seen as a Mother Ireland figure.

Guinevere, Gwenhwyfar

(pronounced like 'gwin + a + vere')

Guinevere is perhaps the best-known heroine in Celtic literature. Her name comes from *gwen* + *hwyfar*, 'fair + smooth' and means 'the fair one'. According to legend, she was the most beautiful woman on earth. She was married to King Arthur but she fell in love with Lancelot and, because of their adultery, the peace of Camelot was shattered. Her story has been told many times and she has often been condemned for destroying the ideal of the Round Table. Her behaviour, though, is not dissimilar to Gráinne's or to that of the many Celtic women who felt that they had a right to personal happiness.

SEE: **Gaynor, Jennifer**

Gunoda (pronounced like 'goon + o + da')

Gunnoda is a Cornish form of Gwyneth, related to *gwyn* and meaning 'blessed'. According to Cornish tradition, Gunnoda was a virgin martyr.

Gwen, Wenn

Cornwall had St Gwen, who was also referred to as Wenn. The name is probably the equivalent of Welsh *gwyn*, meaning 'white, pure, holy'.

SEE: **Aouregwenn, Wenn(a), Winifred, Wynne**

Gwendolen, Gwendolena, Gwendolina, Gwendoline, Gwendolyn

These variants probably come from *gwyn*, 'holy, white', + *dolen*, 'ring', and the name has been popular in Wales, Cornwall and Brittany, where the forms ending in '-a' are preferred. Apart from Saint Gwen, one of the earliest records of the name is to Gwendolena, Merlin's wife.

Gwendydd (pronounced like 'gwen + didh')

Gwendydd is one of the many Welsh names that is abbreviated to Gwen. It means 'morning star' and, since the morning star is the planet Venus, Gwendydd implies great physical beauty.

Gweneira (pronounced like 'gwen + eh + ra')

Gweneira is from *gwen* + *eirwen*, 'pure + snow' and means 'white, pure snow'. It is an attractive name and can, of course, be abbreviated to either Gwen or Eira.

Gwenhwyfar (pronounced like 'gwen + hew + var')

SEE: **Guinevere**

Gwenllian (pronounced like 'gwen + hlee + an')

Gwenllian would be particularly appropriate for a golden-haired baby because this Welsh name comes from *gwen* + *llian* and probably means 'fair + flax' or 'flaxen'.

Gwenonwyn (pronounced like 'gwen + on + win')

Gwenonwyn is a beautiful name meaning 'lily of the valley', a name that used to be applied to the mother of God.

Gwyneth (pronounced like 'gwin + ith')

Gwyneth may be a form of *gwynaeth*, 'luck', or, if it comes from Gwendydd, it may mean 'bliss'.

Gwynne, Gwenn, Gwyn, Gwynn, Gwen, Gwenne, Gwenna, Gwennaig, Winifred, Wynne (pronounced like 'gwin' or 'gwen')

Gwynne comes from *gwyn*, meaning 'fair, white, pure, blessed'. It is more frequently used for a boy than for a girl but it is occasionally used in this way. Gwenn is preferred in Brittany and it also occurs there as Gwenna and Gwennaig.

Hafwen, Hafwyn (pronounced like 'haf + win')

This lovely Welsh name means 'fair summer', from *haf*, 'summer', and *gwyn*, 'white, fair'. It is not widely used at present but could be an attractive present for a summer baby.

Haley, Hayley

This name, which has been popularised by the actress Hayley Mills, may have two possible sources. It may come from Old English and mean 'hay field' or it may come from Gaelic *éalaigh*, 'escape'.

Haude (pronounced like 'ode')

Haude is a Breton name, probably derived from Ada or Adèle and meaning 'noble'. It may also have been influenced by the biblical Adah, meaning 'adornment'. A seventh-century St Ada was abbess at Le Mans.

Heulwen, Heulwyn (pronounced like 'hyool + win' or 'hool + wen')

Heulwen comes from Welsh *heulwen*, meaning 'sunshine'. The equivalent name does not occur in Gaelic. If it did, it would be Soilse from *soilse*, meaning 'brightness, light, sunshine'.

Hieretha (pronounced like 'he + er + ee + tha')

Hieretha is one of a long list of virgin martyrs honoured in Cornwall. Her name probably means 'holy and upright' and she is probably the same saint as Iweryd of Wales

Ia (pronounced like 'ee + a')

Ia was still remembered as a Cornish saint in thirteenth-century records, where she is described as an Irish virgin of noble birth. However, the writer of the record was a Breton cleric and so it is possible that Ia was Breton or Cornish rather than Irish. It is also possible that Ia is a form of *íde*, 'thirst'.

Íde (pronounced like 'eed + deh'), Ida, Ita, Ite

Íde is an Irish name, *íde*, 'thirst (for goodness and knowledge)' and, as one might expect, it was the name of a saint who was closely associated with education. She is linked with Kileedy (*Cill Íde*) in Co. Limerick, according to tradition she was the foster-mother of the infant Jesus. It is occasionally anglicised as Ida (pronounced both as 'I + da' and as 'ee + da') and, in this form, it overlaps with a Germanic Ida, which means 'work' and which was popularised by the Normans. Ida was brought back into fashion by the heroine in Tennyson's poem, *The Princess*. Interestingly, Tennyson's Ida devoted herself to the education of women. The forms Ita and Ite are also used in Ireland as an equivalent of Íde.

Igerna, Igraine (pronounced like 'ee + gerna' and 'ee + grain')

Igerna was the wife of Gorlois of Cornwall. According to legend, she was so beautiful that when Uther Pendragon, the King of Britain, saw her he realised that he could never love another woman. Uther connived with Merlin to visit Igerna in the guise of her husband and they slept together. When Gorlois was killed, Uther and Igerna got married but Uther could never be certain that her son, Arthur, was his. It is not certain what Igerna means but it may be related to Welsh *ynghynn*, 'alight'.

Imogen, Inogen (pronounced like 'im + o + gin' or 'in + o + gin')

The name Imogen was used by Shakespeare in his play, *Cymbeline*, and his character is based on an earlier Inogen or Innogen. It seems probable that Inogen comes from Gaelic *inghean* or *inighion*, meaning 'daughter'. The form with '-m-' may have been influenced by 'image'.

Ineda (pronounced like 'een + ay + da')

Ineda was a Cornish saint, sometimes called Eneda. This name may be from Gaelic *eithne*, 'kernel', or may be related to *aodh*, 'fire, flame'.
SEE: **Enda**

Inira, Inire, Ynyra (pronounced like 'in + eer + a')

These Welsh names mean 'honour' and are the equivalent of Honoria.

Iona (pronounced like 'eye + o + na'), Ione

Iona is the name of a Scottish island that has been adopted for a girl. Its meaning is uncertain but its association with religion makes the name the equivalent of 'blessed'. This usage may have been influenced by the nineteenth-century coinage of Ione, a name meaning 'violet' and meant to conjure up the splendour of Ionian Greece.

Irnan (pronounced like 'eer + nan')
Irnan, whose name may be related to Gaelic *iarann*, 'iron', was one of three sisters with magical powers. It is possible that they were the inspiration for the three 'weird sisters' in *Macbeth*. Irnan had the power to change shapes and challenged Fionn MacCool or any of his champions to a duel.

Iseabeal (pronounced like 'ish + a + bale'), **Iseabeul, Sibéal, Shibley**
These names are based on Isabel, the Spanish form of Elizabeth. All the European versions of the name of John the Baptist's mother come from a Hebrew name, Elisheba, meaning 'God is my oath'. The Irish ending *-béal* and the Scottish ending *-beul* suggest a link with 'mouth' that does not, in fact, exist. The form Sibéal is the result of losing the first syllable. This is an interesting reduction because the Spanish form Isabel had already lost the 'El-' from Elisheba. Shibley is a pet form.
SEE: **Elspeth**

Iseult (pronounced like 'ee + solt'), **Isolde, Isolt, Essyllt, Yseult**
These names are probably all derived from Welsh *Esyllt*, a name that means 'the beautiful one'. There are several Iseults in literature but we shall mention only two: Iseult of Ireland and Iseult of Brittany. The first was the wife of Mark of Cornwall but she fell in love with Tristan, her husband's nephew. They became lovers but when Mark discovered the affair, he banished Tristan to Brittany. Tristan eventually married Iseult of Brittany because he believed that his first love was beyond his reach. When Iseult of Ireland heard that he was dying, she went to Brittany. She arrived too late to save him and died so that they could be together in the afterlife.
SEE: **Tristan**

Isla (pronounced like 'I'll + a')
Isla is the name of a Scottish river that has been adopted as a girl's name. The meaning is uncertain but it may be related to *aileach*, 'rocky place'.

Ita
SEE: **Íde**

Ivori, Ivory (pronounced like 'I + for + ee')
This is occasionally used as the female equivalent of Welsh Ivor or Ifor, which probably comes from Scandinavian *yr* + *herr*, 'yew' + 'army'.
SEE: **Ifor, Ivor**

The letter 'j' was not used in the early Celtic alphabets, and so only a few Celtic names begin with it.

Jennifer, Jenniver
Jennifer or Jenniver is a Cornish form of Guinevere, which comes from *gwen* + *hwyfar*, 'fair + smooth',

implying 'very beautiful'. One hundred years ago, this name was virtually unknown outside Cornwall, but it is now widely used throughout the world in its full form and also as Jeni, Jenni and Jenny.

SEE: Guinevere

Jocelyn (pronounced like 'joss + el + linn')

Jocelyn was originally a boy's name, like Evelyn and Hilary, but it is now almost exclusively used for a girl. Its origins are probably mixed. It may come from an old German name, meaning 'connected with the Goths'. It certainly seems to have been used by the Normans in the form Joscelin. It is equally possible, however, that Jocelyn is a diminutive of Joyce, which is from *Judocus*, a latinised form of *iod*, 'lord'.

Joyce

It has often been suggested that Joyce comes from Old French *joir*, 'to be joyous, happy', and it is likely that the Norman use of such a verb reinforced the name. It is more probable, however, that Joyce comes from the seventh-century Breton hermit and saint, Judoc. His name may be from *Judocus*, a latinised form of *iod*, 'lord'. In the past, Joyce was usually a boy's name but at the moment it is exclusively female. It is quite a common surname and is known worldwide because of the writings of James Joyce.

Judwara, Juthwara (pronounced like 'jood + wara' and 'jooth + wara')

St Judwara was a virgin martyr, much admired for her generosity of spirit and for the power of her intercession. Her name is likely to come from *iod* and mean 'ruler, lord' but it may also have been influenced by the Hebrew male name, Judah, which means 'praised' and by the female equivalent, Judith. Judith was the name of a niece of William the Conqueror and so could have encouraged the popularity of Judwara.

Kacee, Kaci, Kasey (pronounced like 'kay + see')

These are variants of Gaelic *cathasach*, 'vigilant, alert in war'. They are modern forms of Casey.

Kady, Kaydi, Kaydy (pronounced like 'kay + dee')

It is possible that this name has been taken over from the town in Northern Ireland or that it is a modern spelling of *céadach*, meaning 'first' and could imply 'first child' or 'first in favour'.

Kalin, Kaylin (pronounced like 'kay + lin')

SEE: **Keelin**

Kaitlin, Kaitlyn, Kaytlin, Kaytlyn

These are recent spellings of Caitlin, a form of Catherine, which is related to Greek *katharos*, 'pure'. They are almost exclusively American and are usually pronounced like 'Kate + Lynn'.

SEE: **Kathleen**

Karel

Karel is a Breton name, related to Carol, and coming from Carola, a female form of Charles, which probably comes from a Germanic *carl*, meaning 'man' or 'strong'. The Breton form may have been influenced by the Irish surname 'Carroll', which may come from *cearbh*, 'elk' .

Karen, Kevan, Kevin

SEE: **Cairenn, Karel**

Katell

Katell is a Breton form of the Greek-inspired name Catherine, from *katharos*, 'pure, clear'. The Celts all seem to have used a form with 'l' as well as a form with 'r', and so we have both Caitlín and Caitriona.

SEE: **Caitlín**

Kathleen

Kathleen has been used so often for Irish girls that it has become almost a generic name for Irish girls away from home, as in the ballad:

I'll take you home again, Kathleen,
Across the ocean wild and wide
To where your heart has ever been
Since first you were my bonnie bride.

It is an Irish form of Catherine and the 'k' spelling is an anglicisation, since there was no 'k' in the Irish alphabet. The meaning of the name goes back to Greek *katharos*, 'pure'.

SEE: **Caitlín**

Kaytlin, Kaytlyn

SEE: **Caitlín**

Kean, Cian (pronounced like 'keen' or 'kee + an')

Kean has been adopted in parts of the Americas, including the Caribbean, as a girl's name. It comes from *cian* and means 'ancient' and implies 'seniority, the wisdom of age'. It is likely that Kean has been adopted from the surname Kean(e), rather than directly from the warrior hero, Cian, who was Brian Boru's son-in-law.

SEE: **Cian**

Keela (pronounced like 'kee + la'), Keeley, Keeli, Keely (pronounced like 'kee + lee'), Kyla (pronounced like 'kie + la')

The Gaelic word *cadhla* is found mainly in poetry and means 'so beautiful that only poets can describe her'. It is the sort of name that any little girl could be proud of.

Keelin (pronounced like 'kee + lin'), Caoilfhin(n) (pronounced like 'kale + in')

This lovely name is underused. It comes from two Gaelic adjectives, *caol*, 'slender', and *finn*, 'white, fair, pure'. The name is occasionally pronounced like 'kaolin', the fine white clay that is used in the manufacture of china and medicines. (This word comes from *Kaoling*, a mountain in China that means 'high hill'.)

SEE: **Caoilfhinn**

Keenan

Keenan is probably a diminutive of 'Kean', coming from *cian*. It is quite a common surname and is being used as a first name for both daughters and sons.

SEE: **Kean**

Keera, Keira (pronounced like 'key + ra')

SEE: **Ciara**

Kelly

Kelly is currently popular worldwide as a name for both girls and boys. As a surname, it has been associated quintessentially with Ireland, although it also occurs in the Isle of Man.

The surname may come from *ceallach* and may mean 'hermit' or *ceallúir*, 'churchyard', suggesting perhaps 'steady church-goer'. The meanings of 'red-haired' and 'strife' have also been suggested. (The Kelly family was renowned for its quick temper and its courage in battle.)

Kendra (pronounced like 'ken + dra')

Kendra is a relatively recent creation. It may be a female form of Kendrick, meaning 'wise ruler', or it may be a combination of *ceann*, 'head' +

Sandra, a form of Alexandra, and thus mean 'helper of people'.

Kerenza

This lovely Cornish name is related to Welsh *car* and Gaelic *cara* and means 'love, little love'. It is not widely used at present but could easily become popular in the future.

Keri, Kerye

This is the name of a Cornish saint. It is probably related to Welsh Ceri and means 'love'.

Keri, Kerri, Kerry

Many children of Irish descent have been given this name, especially if a parent or grandparent came from Kerry. The county probably means 'country of the Ciaraidhde' or 'country of the children of Ciar' and *ciar* meant 'dark' and probably implied 'dark hair and brown eyes'.

SEE: **Ceri, Ciara**

Kew

Most people who hear this name probably think of Kew Gardens, in London, but Kew or Kewe was a Cornish saint. We know virtually nothing about her but the name may be a form of Hugh, which means 'heart' or it may be related to Welsh *cyw*, meaning 'chick'.

Keyne, Keynwir (pronounced like 'keen' and 'keen + wir')

Keyne was a Cornish saint, possibly one of the many children of St Brechan and St Gladuse. Keyne was remembered particularly because she had the wonderfully useful talent of turning serpents into stones, which could then be used to build walls. It is not certain what her name means but it may be related to *canny* and imply 'knowledgeable'. St Keyne was honoured for her knowledge of cures and medicines.

Keyra
SEE: **Ciara**

Kiaran
Kiaran is an anglicised spelling of Ciarán, from *ciar*, 'dark', meaning 'little dark one'. This name used to be exclusively male but it is now also being used for girls.
SEE: **Ciara, Ciarán**

Kiera, Kira, Kyra (pronounced like 'key + ra')
This spelling is sometimes used as a female form of Ciarán and means 'little dark one'.
SEE: **Ciara**

Kirstie, Kirsty
Kirstie is a Scottish form of Christina and means 'Christian, follower of Christ'. It is not, therefore, a Celtic name but this form certainly seems to have originated in Scotland.

Kodi, Kody
See: **Codi**

Koulm, Koulmia (pronounced like 'cool + em' and 'cool + me + a')
These are Breton names. The first is a female form of *columba*, 'dove', and the second means 'little dove'.

SEE: **Columba, Colm**

Kristell, Krystell
See: **Crystal**

Kyara
SEE: **Ciara**

Kyla
SEE: **Keela**

Kylie (pronounced like 'kile + ee')
Kylie is said to be an Australian Aboriginal word, meaning 'boomerang', and undoubtedly, it may have this meaning for most Australian parents. It has, however, also been used as a pet form of Kyle, which may come from the Gaelic words *cill*, 'church' or *coill*, 'wood'.

Kyna (pronounced like 'key + na')
Kyna seems to be a modern name based on Gaelic *cion*, 'love, affection', or on *cíoná*, 'best, champion, star'.

Kyra
SEE: **Kira**

Laban
Yeats writes about Laban, the sister of Fand and wife of Manannan Mac Lír, the god of the sea. Her name may be related to *lábán*, meaning 'soft earth'. One of her jobs was to look after a well so that all the animals might have clean water. She neglected the well and was punished by being transformed into an otter.

Lachtna (pronounced like 'locked + na' or 'locht + na')

Lachtna could, in theory, be used for a boy or a girl. It is related to *lachtacht*, 'milkiness', and means 'pure as milk'. It could refer to fair skin or to a child that would be a source of goodness to others.

Lana

Lana is probably a shortened form of Alana, from *a leanbh* and meaning 'darling'. It was popularised by Lana Turner, the Hollywood actress.

Laorans (pronounced like 'law + rance')

Laorans is a Breton female form of Laurence. Its nearest English equivalent would be Laura, which comes from Latin *larus*, 'laurel'.

Lasair (pronounced like 'lass + air')

Lasair comes from Gaelic *lasair*, 'flame, blaze of fire or sunlight', and is thus an attractive name, especially for a redhead.

Lena, Lenaig

Helen was adopted by the Bretons in the forms of Lena, Lenaig and Elena. All of the variants come from Greek *helios*, 'sun', and suggest 'sunbeam, ray of light'.

SEE: **Aileen**

Lesley

Lesley is of Scottish origin and comes from the lands of Lesslyn, a place-name that probably means 'grey fort' or 'protector of the grey fort'. The ending '-ley' is used for a girl and Leslie is preferred for a boy.

Liadán, Liadhain, Liadin

Liadán, or occasionally Liadin, was a poet and considered to be extraordinarily beautiful. Her name comes from *liath*, 'grey', and means 'grey lady' or 'grey poet' but there was nothing 'grey' about her behaviour. When Cuirithir, another poet, saw her, he fell madly in love with her and marvelled at the thought of the perfect children they would have. Liadán, however, had other ideas. It is quite possible that she was already a nun.

SEE: **Cuirithír**

Liban (pronounced like 'lee + ban')

Liban was the wife of Labraidh and her name may include *bean*, 'woman', or it may come from *lúbán*, meaning 'loop, net'. When her husband's kingdom was in jeopardy, she sought Cúchulainn's help. She offered him the hand of her sister-in-law in marriage, in return.

Linet, Luned, Lunet, Lynette

Linet was a Celtic character, reputed to have lived at the time of King Arthur. She had magical powers, which she used to rescue brave warriors who were imprisoned or held hostage. Her name may be a diminutive of *linn*, 'pool, waterfall', or *llyn*, 'lake'. It has merged with Lynette, which may mean 'little lake' or may, in some cases, be a diminutive form of Lynda.

SEE: **Liban**

Loreto, Loretta, Lori

Loreto is a placename in Italy that has, for almost a millennium, been associated with the house of Nazareth in which Jesus grew up. It is used widely in Ireland and is a good name for children with travelling ambitions, in that Our Lady of Loreto is the patroness of aviators. Mother Teresa of Calcutta was trained by the Irish Sisters of Loreto.

The name Laura, which came from Latin *laurus* and meant 'laurel wreath', gave rise to the diminutive Lauretta and Loretta. The pet form Lori is becoming popular and has become a name in its own right.

Luisiúil (pronounced like 'louiss + shoo + ell')

Luisiúil comes from Irish Gaelic *luisiúil*, meaning 'radiant, glowing'. It is thus related in meaning to Latin *lux*, 'light', and offers an attractive alternative to Lucy or Lucia.

Luned, Lunet, Lynette

SEE: **Linet**

Mab

Mab may well be a reduced form of Madhbh and thus mean 'one who can cause great joy'. Alternatively, it may come from Welsh *maban*, 'child'. Shakespeare uses the name of Mab for the queen of the fairies in *A Midsummer Night's Dream*. Mab is an attractive name for a child and is sometimes used as an abbreviation of

Mabel, which comes, in fact from Old French *amabel*, and means 'loving, amiable'.

Maban, Maben, Mabin, Mabon, Mabyn (pronounced like 'mab + in')

This name almost certainly comes from Welsh *maban*, meaning 'child'. St Maban was a Cornish saint and is reputed to have lived a life of extraordinary sanctity in the north-east of the country.

Macha (pronounced like 'moh + ha' or 'mock +a')

There are several women of this name in Irish tradition and the name is so old that its meaning is uncertain. It may, however, be related to *machaire*, 'a plain', or, in her guise as goddess of war, it may be related to *macht*, a literary word for 'slaughter'. The goddess Macha lived as a human wife in Ulster until her husband Crunnchú boasted that his pregnant wife could run faster than the king's best horse. Macha's name is still found in the name Armagh, from *Árd Mhacha*, 'high Macha'.

SEE: **Crunnchú**

Madhbh, Maebh, Maeve, Mave, Meadhbh, Medb(h), Meibh (pronounced like 'mayv')

Madhbh, whose name is usually anglicised to Maeve, was the great warrior queen of Connacht. Her name may be related to *mab*, 'child', or to *meisce* and mean 'the cause of great joy' or 'the cause of great intoxication'. She was a woman of strong views. She left King Conchubhar for Ailill, whom she married and then quarrelled with over which of them had the greater herd of cows. Madhbh's exploits are recorded in *Táin Bó Cualigne*, 'The Cattle Raid of Cooley', in which she goes to war with Ulster in order to gain the great brown bull owned by Daire.

Madrun (pronounced like 'mad + roon')

Madrun is a Cornish saint whose name may have been inspired by Madeleine, the French form of Magdalene, after Mary of Magdala in St Luke's Gospel. She is widely regarded as being the repentant sinner who washed Christ's feet with her tears and dried them with her hair.

Maeve, Mave
SEE: **Madhbh**

Mailli, Melle (pronounced like 'may + lee' or 'mel + ée')

Mailli is a Cornish form of Mary that may have given rise to Molly. Melle is a variant that still occurs in Brittany.

Máire, Mair, Mairi, Maisre, Mara, Mari, Maria, Mariam, Marie, Mary, Marya, Maura, May, Melle, Miriam, Moira, Moya

It seems likely that Christ's mother was called Mariam (a variant of Miriam) and that translators from Latin thought of it as the accusative form of 'Maria', a name that she certainly did not have. Nobody knows the exact meaning of Mariam or Miriam, although it may be related to 'bitterness, sorrow' and therefore be appropriate that Simeon should tell her in Luke, 2:35: 'And thine own heart a sword shall pierce.'

The name that was used in Ireland for Our Lady was *Muire*, a form that still occurs in the Irish version of the Hail Mary: *S'é do bheatha, a Mhuire*. Her name was so honoured that it was rarely used as a child's name in Celtic communities until the end of the fifteenth century. (The early Celts would have felt as awkward about giving a daughter the name Muire as they still would about giving a son the name Jesus.) They did, however, adopt other forms of Mariam and so today we find all the above as well as such diminutives as Maisie, Mamie, Maureen, Molly and Moyenna.

Mairéad, Mairead, Maighread, Mairighead, Muiréad (pronounced like 'ma + raid')

These are Irish forms of Margaret, which comes from Greek *margaron*, 'pearl'. It was probably borrowed into Gaelic in Norman times from the French form Marguerite. The name has been held by many saints, including St Margaret of Antioch, who was specially honoured in France. Indeed, St Joan of Arc insisted at her trial that St Margaret spoke to her and advised her on how to save France. St Margaret's emblem is a dragon, a symbol that links her to Wales. Occasionally, in Northern Ireland Mairighead is pronounced like 'mar + a + gid'. The diminutives Meg and Peg as well as Meigín and Peigín are also used.

Malvina (pronounced like 'mal + veen + a')

James Macpherson created the name Malvina in his fictional 'translation' of an Irish bard called Ossian. The name happens to be almost identical in form to the Argentine name for the Falklands, the Malvinas, but Macpherson could have got the name from *maol* + *Mhena*, pronounced Malvena and meaning 'the follower of Mena'.

Maolíosa (pronounced like 'mwel + eesa'), **Melissa**

This beautiful name has two possible sources. The first is from *maol* + *Íosa*, 'devotee of Jesus', a name that could be either male or female. The second could be from the Celtic words for honey. Welsh has *mel* and Gaelic has *mil*. Legends abound of saints who were beekeepers so the name might have started as a nickname.

Mara, Mari, Maria, Mariam, Marie, Mary, Marya, Maura
SEE: **Máire**

Maureen, Maurene, Maurine, Móirín

Maureen comes from Gaelic *Móirín*, meaning 'little Mary'. It is thus a diminutive but has for centuries been regarded as a name in its own right.
SEE: **Máire**

Mavis, Mavourna, Mavourneen (pronounced like 'may + vis', 'ma + vorna' and 'ma + vorn + een')

These names come from Gaelic *mo mhuirnín*, 'my little darling' and the forms could also have been influenced by Muire and French *mavis*, a name that means 'singing bird, thrush'. Mavis seems to have been borrowed into French from Breton.

May
SEE: **Máire**

Meadhbh, Medb(h), Meibh
SEE: **Madhbh**

Meara (pronounced like 'meer + a')

This is occasionally used as a first name. It may be another form of Mary or a borrowing from the surname Ó Meara and thus it could be related to *mara*, 'sea' or 'flexibility'. Either way, it is an attractive name.

Medwenna, Modwen(na), Morwyn(na) (pronounced like 'med + wenna', 'mod + wen(na)' and 'mor + win')

These are probably all variations of the Welsh *morwyn*, maiden, and thus indirectly names associated with the Blessed Virgin Mary.

Megan, Meghan (pronounced like 'meg + an'), **Meg**

Megan is a Welsh diminutive form of

Margaret, from Greek *margaron*, 'pearl', and thus means 'little pearl'. The form may have been borrowed from, or given rise to such abbreviated forms of Margaret as Meg, Maggie and Mags.

Melanie

Melanie comes from a Greek adjective *melas*, meaning 'black, dark'. It was the name of two fifth- century saints. The name was rarely used outside Cornwall until this cen- tury and it was popular there because it overlapped with the Celtic prefix mal or mel, meaning 'devotee of a saint'.

Melissa
SEE: **Maolíosa**

Melle (pronounced like 'mel + lih' or 'mel')

This is a Breton form of Mary. The substitution of 'l' for 'r' is found in many languages, including English, where we find both Mary and Molly.
SEE: **Máire**

Mena

In most families, Mena is an abbreviated form of Philomena, a name that probably comes from Latin *filla luminae*, 'daughter of light', although it may have been influenced by the Greek word for 'nightingale'. According to Cornish traditions, however, there was a Celtic saint, Mena, about whom little is known.

Meredith, Meredyth, Meredydd, Merideth (pronounced like 'mer + id + ith')

The Welsh surname, Meredith, meaning 'great lord' comes from the given name Maredudd. Meredith was originally only given to boys but is perhaps now more frequently a girl's name. The name is occasionally shortened to Merry, which is certainly a cheerful abbreviation for a lively little girl, with sufficient overlap with Mary to make it acceptable.

Merewin, Merewenna, Mervena

Merewin was a Cornish saint and her name is found in all of the above forms. It probably comes from *morwyn*, maiden, like Welsh Medwenna. It is also possible that Mervena is a form of Marvin, or *myrddyn*, meaning 'famous friend'.

Merlene, Merlyn, Muirgheal (pronounced like 'mer + leen', 'mer + 'lin' and 'mwir + yal')

Merlene is probably a form of Marilyn, which is a blend of Mary + Lynn. Merlyn may have the same source or come from Merlin. They could also be diminutives of Irish *muirgheal*, a lovely name that means 'bright, clear as the sea'.

Merrill
SEE: **Muirgheal**

Meryl, Muirgheal, Murel, Muriel

These names may come from Muirgheal, 'clear as the sea', or from Welsh Muriel, 'bright as the sea'.

However, the forms and the meanings are so close that we may simply have two forms of the one Celtic name. Meryl has possibly been influenced by the French word *merle*, 'blackbird', and the name has been popularised by the Hollywood actress Meryl Streep.

SEE: **Muirgheal**

Miniver

Greer Garson once acted in a film as Mrs Miniver, but the use of Miniver as a given name in Cornwall predates this by over a thousand years. Miniver might be a regional form of Guinevere, *gwen* + *hwyfar*, 'fair + smooth' and meaning 'very beautiful', or it may be derived from Minerva, the Roman goddess of wisdom. In this case, the name would imply 'wise one'. Cornish people tell an interesting story about St Miniver that links her with the Irish banshee. Apparently, Miniver was sitting at her well minding her own business and combing her hair when the devil tried to tempt her. She threw her comb at the devil and he had to turn into a rock to avoid being hit. In some Irish traditions, the banshee combs her hair as she wails, and if she throws her comb at someone and it strikes, then that person will die within the space of a three – whether three days, weeks or months.

Miriam
SEE: **Máire**

Modwenna
SEE: **Medwenna**

Moina (pronounced like 'moy + na')

Moina is said to be a variant of Myrna, but this has a very New York ring to it:

> They say the boid is on the wing
> but that's absoid
> Because the wing is on the boid!

It is more likely that it is related to Gaelic *móinín*, 'soft, grassy patch'.

SEE: **Myrna**

Moira
SEE: **Máire**

Molly
SEE: **Máire**

Mona, Monenna

The name Mona is probably more widely used in Ireland than elsewhere and it is an attractive name, capable of being pronounced without difficulty all over the world. Like a number of simple names, its origins are unclear. It may come from Gaelic *Muadhnaid* or *Muadnait* and mean 'noble'; it may have been influenced by the Norman name Monique, 'giver of advice', and it is occasionally used as an abbreviated form of Monica; it may have come from a reduced form of Madonna, 'lady', as in the Mona Lisa; it may even have come from Arabic Mona or Maimona; and finally, it may be from a personification of the moon as Mona.

Mor (pronounced like 'more')
Mor was a goddess whose name meant 'great one'. Her descendants became the kings and queens of Munster.

Morag (pronounced like 'more + ag')
Morag is a Scottish form of *mór* meaning 'great' plus the ending *ag/óg*, meaning 'young' and so implying 'great young one'. It was virtually unheard of outside Scotland until this century but, like Kirsty, it has become extremely popular throughout the English-speaking world.

Morgan, Morgana, Morganez, Morgane, Morganna, Morrigan

Morgan probably comes from Welsh and may mean either 'great queen' or 'bright sea'. The original Morgan or Morrighan was a goddess of war, but one of the best-known Morgans was Morgan le Fay, the daughter of the king of Cornwall. She was an implacable enemy of King Arthur and tried to put an end to his reign. Morgan was sometimes dismissed as a witch, but her name and her fame have gradually been restored. Morgan is used mainly in America but Morgana has been found in England, Morrigan in Northern Ireland and the forms Morganez and Morgane are still current in Brittany. The American actress Morgan Brittany is likely to increase the name's popularity.

Morna
SEE: **Muirne, Myrna**

Morwenna, Morwyn (pronounced like 'mor + wenna' and 'mor + win')
This name was used in Cornwall and seems to be either a variant of Morgan and thus to mean 'great queen', or a form of Welsh *morwyn*, 'maiden'. It is being used again in Cornwall, after a gap of almost 1500 years.
SEE: **Medwenna, Morgan**

Moya, Moyenna
Moya is a variant of Máire but it has been used so widely that it has gained the status of a name in its own right. Moyenna is like a blend of Moya and either Anna, meaning 'graceful', or Enya, meaning 'flame'.
SEE: **Máire**

Muirgheal, Muriel, Merrill
Muriel may come from the Irish name Muirgheal, meaning 'bright as the sea', or from Welsh *mor*, 'sea' + *can*, 'bright', an almost identical meaning. The name was popular throughout the Celtic regions in the Middle Ages, but gradually fell from favour. The variants Merrill or, less commonly, Merell, and Mirielle, are again becoming popular.

Muirne, Murine (pronounced like 'moor + nyih' and 'moor + een')
Murine, which may be from *muirne*, 'beloved', or *mathair* + *Fionn*, meaning 'mother of Fionn', was the

sister-in-law of Lugh and the mother of Fionn MacCool. She gave birth to Fionn after the death of her husband and left the child in the care of a female druid and a female warrior.
SEE: **Myrna**

Murphy

Murphy is an Irish surname from *muir + cú* meaning 'hound of the sea'. It was originally a nickname, then a first name, a surname, and now a given name again. Until recently, it was only given to boys, but the chief character in the American TV series *Murphy Brown* is a woman, Candice Bergen.

Mwynen (pronounced like 'mwin + in')

This Welsh name means 'my gentle one' and is related to the adjective *addfwyn*, 'gentle'. It is less widely used than Welsh names such as Olwen, but it may become more popular because of its meaning.

Myfanwy (pronounced like 'mif + an + wee')

Myfanwy is Welsh and means 'my lovely little one'. It is still relatively rare outside Wales but looks attractive and has a lovely meaning.

Myrna

Myrna is almost certainly from Irish *múirne*, meaning 'darling, beloved'. It was popularised by the Hollywood star Myrna Loy.
SEE: **Moira**

Náible, Nápla (pronounced like 'naub + la' or 'naup + la')

The Normans introduced the name Annabel into Ireland, probably in the forms Amabel, Anable, Anaple, all of which are related to *aimable*, 'beloved, lovable'. The initial vowel was lost in Irish and Náible and Nápla became popular.

Nan, Nana, Nanna

Nanna is one of the words like 'Mama' that occur in virtually every culture. It is sometimes used in Ireland as a form of Áine and can also be related to *naonúr*, 'nine'. However, Nan(n)a was also an ancient goddess of flowers and this fact may have influenced the popularity of Nan(n)a.

Navlin, Newlyn (pronounced like 'nav + lin' or 'new + lin')

This name may be a blend of *naomh*, 'holy' + *linn*, 'pool', and would thus be linked to the Celtic interest in healing waters.
SEE: **Nuline**

Neala, Neila, Neilla, Nelda, Nilda

These are feminine forms of Neal and Neil(l), which are modern variants of Niall. It means 'female champion' and has been used in America, especially by people whose ancestors came from Northern Ireland, where Neal, Neill, McNeill

and O'Neill occur frequently as surnames.
SEE: **Niall**

Néamh (pronounced like 'nee + iv')
SEE: **Niamh**

Nemetona (pronounced like 'nem + et + ona')
Nemetona was a goddess who takes her name from her function. She was the 'keeper of the sacred grove' and her name may include *naomh*, 'holy'. Oak groves and hawthorn groves were sacred to the Celts and many of the druidic rituals were performed inside them.

Nerys (pronounced like 'ner + iss')
Nerys is the female form of Welsh *ner*, 'lord', and thus means 'lady'. It became popular in this century, first in Wales and then in various parts of the world. The actress Nerys Hughes helped to popularise the name in the late 60s, when she acted in the award-winning series, *The Liver Birds*.

Nessa, Neasa
Nessa was the wife of Cathbad and the mother of Conchubar. Her name was originally *Assa*, meaning 'gentle', but, to defend her people, she took up arms against Cathbad and was so successful that her name was changed to *Ní Assa*, 'not gentle'. Later, she cajoled her second husband, Fergus, into giving up his kingdom to his stepson, Conchubar, for a year, but Conchubar ruled so

wisely and so well that the people refused to let him return the kingdom to Fergus.

Nesta
Nesta may be a latinised form of Nest, the Welsh pet form of Agnes, which comes from Greek *hagnos*, meaning 'pure, holy'. The 'h' from *hagnos* was lost when the name was equated with Latin *agnus*, meaning 'lamb'. Nest ap Tudor was the wife of Gerald of Windsor and mother of Maurice FitzGerald, and therefore mother of all the FitzGeralds.
SEE: **Oanez**

Nevidd, Nevidh, Nevydd (pronounced like 'nev + id')
Nevid(d) is a Celtic word for 'sacred place' and it seems to have been used as a woman's name in both Cornwall and Wales, where the church of Llanyfydd was called after her.

Newlyn
SEE: **Navlin**

Niamh (pronounced like 'nee + iv' or 'neev')
Niamh of the Golden Hair was the daughter of Manannan, the god of the sea. She was extraordinarily beautiful and could have had any god she wanted. However, she fell in love with Fionn's son, Oisín, and took him to live with her in Tír na-nÓg, where 300 years passed as if it were a few weeks. Her name, *niamh*, means 'radiance, brightness' and it is close

in form to *naomh*, the Irish word for 'saint'.

Nodhlaig(ín), Nollaig(ín) (pronounced like 'null + ig (+ een)')

These are words that mean 'Christmas' and are the equivalent of Noelle. Nodhlaig comes ultimately from Latin *natalis dies Domini*, 'birthday of the Lord'. The diminutives Nodhlaigín or Nollaigín are also popular.

Nola, Noleen, Nolwenn

Nola and Noleen are usually considered to be abbreviated forms of Fin(n)ola, a variant of Fionnuala. They may come from a Celtic name *nola*, 'famous', and are similar to the Breton saint's name, Nolwenn, whose feast is celebrated on 6 July.

SEE: **Fionnuala, Nuala**

Noni, Nonie (pronounced like 'no + nee')

Noni(e) is a pet form of Nora in Ireland but has been used elsewhere as a form of Ione, a name that was created in the nineteenth century in deference to Ionian Greek culture.

SEE: **Nora**

Nonn, Nonna, Nonita

Nonn occurs in both Cornwall and Brittany but the variants Nonna and Nonita seem to be limited to Cornwall. It is possible that the name means 'ninth', either a ninth daughter or a ninth child, or it may simply mean 'nun'.

SEE: **Enid**

Nora, Norah, Noreen

Nora is a shortened form of Latin *Honora*, 'honour', and became so popular in Ireland that many people assumed it was Irish. The form 'Norah' was influenced by such Biblical names as Sarah. Noreen is a blend of Nora and the Irish diminutive marker -*ín* and so means 'little honourable one'.

Nuala (pronounced like 'noo + ala')

Although Nuala is really a shortened form of Fionnuala, it is widely used as a name in its own right. It means 'fair shouldered, exceptionally lovely'.

SEE: **Fionnuala**

Nuline

Nuline is probably a Cornish form of Newlyn, although it may also be a diminutive of Nola and mean 'famous little one'.

SEE: **Navlín, Nola**

Oanez (pronounced like 'wan + ez')

Oanez is a Breton form of Agnes, a name that came originally from Greek *hagnos*, 'pure, holy', and was reinforced by Latin *agnus*, 'lamb'. Variants of Agnes were popular throughout the Celtic regions because of the legends of St Agnes, a thirteen-year-old martyr. She wanted to give herself to God and when a young man tried to ravish her, she was protected by an angel.

SEE: **Nesta**

Oberon

Oberon was the king of the fairies in Shakespeare's *A Midsummer Night's Dream*. It is not clear where the name comes from or what it means. It is sometimes spelt Auberon and associated with French *aube*, 'dawn', or a German name meaning 'noble'. Another alternative is that it is an anglicisation of O'Brien, meaning 'descendant of the noble one'. It is certainly an attractive name and was used as a surname by the Hollywood actress Merle Oberon, a fact that has encouraged the name's association with girls.

Odhrán, Oran, Orin, Orna

(pronounced like 'o + ran' or 'or + na')

These names are all variants of *odhra*, meaning 'dark haired'. Like so many old Irish names, there are several saints called Orna and one of them may have established a Christian settlement in Iona before Columbanus went there.

Olwen, Olwyn, Olwynne

(pronounced like 'ol + win')

Olwen is a Welsh name from *ol + gwen*, 'footprint + white'. According to one legend, Olwen was the daughter of a giant called Yspaddadyn and was so beautiful that white clover grew wherever she put her foot. As might be expected, many men wanted to marry her and they had to perform many well-nigh impossible tasks before her father would allow her to leave home.

Oona(gh) (pronounced like 'ou + na')

Oona or Oonagh is a variant of Una. The name may come from Latin *una*, 'one (female)' and it is sometimes used as an Irish form of Unity.

SEE: **Úna**

Orchil(l) (pronounced like 'or + hill')

Orchil was a Fomorian goddess associated with the coming of nightfall. Her name may be related to *ortha*, 'prayer' or it may come from *odhra* and mean 'dark-haired'.

SEE: **Odhrán**

Orfhlaith
SEE: **Orla**

Orin

It was been suggested that Orin is a form of Latin Oriana, 'the golden one'. Certainly, it could be a diminutive of Gaelic *ór*, 'gold', although it could also be a form of *odhra*, 'dark haired'.

Orla, Órla, Órfhlaith, Orlaith

(pronounced like 'or + la')

Orla means 'golden lady' and the attractive meaning helps to explain the current popularity of the name. Orla could also come from *ór*, 'golden' + *snaith*, 'thread'.

Orna
SEE: **Odhrán**

Pádraigín, Paidrigín, Paddy, Paití, Patricia, Pat, Patsy (pronounced like 'paw + drig + een')

These names are female versions of Padraig and Patrick, both forms of *patricius*, 'of noble birth'. Since the name Patricius was Latin, not Celtic, it is not surprising that non-Irish Patricias exist. The pet names Paddy, Paití, Pat and Patsy are perhaps even more common in Ireland than Patricia. Pádraigín is traditionally a boy's name which has become increasingly a girl's name this century.

SEE: **Padraic**

Peggy, Peig, Peigín (pronounced like 'peg', 'peg + een')

These names are usually described as forms of Margaret, coming from Greek *margaros*, meaning 'pearl'. The reasons for including them in a dictionary like this are two-fold. First, Peggy and Maggie are extremely popular in Ireland, the Isle of Man and Scotland; and secondly, the shift between 'p' and 'm' is unusual in English. It only occurs with Peggy and Maggie and Polly and Molly. Such a shift is much less unusual in Welsh where 'm' may be a mutation of 'p'.

Piala (pronounced like 'pea + a + la')

According to the Breton cleric and historian, Anselm, Piala was a saint who was martyred in Cornwall, but he does not make clear whether she was Breton or Cornish. The meaning of her name is also uncertain but it may be related to Welsh *pwyll*, 'prudence'. Certainly, the name Prudence was popular among Cornish and Devonian Puritans.

Polly

Polly, like Molly, is a form of Mary.

SEE: **Máire, Peggy**

Proinséas, Pronsaisín (pronounced like 'pron + shee + iss' and 'pron + shee + iss + een')

These names are both based on Frances and are usually given as a mark of respect to St Francis of Assisi, a saint who remains popular in Ireland. The form with '-*ín*' is sometimes translated as Frankie.

SEE: **Proinsias**

The early Celtic alphabets did not use 'q' and so it is unusual in Celtic names. It does, however, occur as an alternative spelling for the initial cluster 'kw' as in 'Quinn'.

Queenie
SEE: **Quinnie**

Quillane

Quillane is probably a female form of the surname Quillen or McQuillen but its choice may have been helped by the existence of the noun *cúileann*, 'fair maiden'.

Quinnie

Quinnie has been used as a female form of Quinn, which probably comes from the name Conn, meaning 'intelligence'. It can also be a variant of Kinnie, a Breton name associated with the defeat of darkness over light. Her feast day is celebrated, like St Brigid's, on 1 February. Occasionally, Queenie is used.

Radha (pronounced like 'row + a')
Radha has become popular in Ireland, possibly because of its link with *radharc*, 'vision'. The name may also be related to *ruadh*, 'red', and so would be a perfect choice for a red-headed vision.

Raghnailt, Raghnaid (pronounced like 'rye + nelt' and 'rye + nidge')
The Celts borrowed Randall, meaning 'wolf shield', from the Vikings. The feminine form Raghnailt has been used in Ireland and the Isle of Man, while the Scots prefer Raghnaid. The name has been linked to Rachel, Regina and Rona, and it may well have contributed to the popularity of all of these names.

Regan

Regan may be used for either a girl or a boy. It comes from *rí*, 'sovereign, king' and means 'the king's child'. Shakespeare used the name for one of the daughters in *King Lear*, but the name itself is attractive and may be related to or derived from the Irish surname O'Re(a)gan, which means 'descendant of a king'.

Rhedyn (pronounced like 'hred + in')
Rhedyn, or *rhedynen*, is Welsh for 'fern'. It is doubly attractive nowadays because of its Welsh origin and also because it is linked to the vogue for nature names, such as Daisy, Poppy and Rose. For people with a Classical bent, the name is reminiscent of Greek *Rhea*, the name of the mother of the gods and with a meaning of 'poppy'.

Rhian (pronounced like 'hree + an')
This abbreviated form of *rhiannon*, 'nymph', is likely to become a name in its own right.

Rhiannon, Riwanon (pronounced like 'hree + an + on' and 'ree + wan + on')
Rhiannon is Welsh and means 'nymph' or 'moon goddess'. She is sometimes also called Rigantona, 'great queen'. In Welsh literature, Rhiannon was the daughter of the king of the Underworld. She was exceptionally beautiful as well as being a fine horsewoman. Pwyll wanted her as his wife but was tricked into handing Rhiannon over to Gwawl. Rhiannon, however, did not want Gwawl. She showed Pwyll how Gwawl could be outwitted, and so she was able to marry the man of her

choice. The Breton form of the name is Riwanon.

Rhianwen (pronounced like 'hree + an + win')

Rhianwen is from Welsh *rhiain* + *gwen* and means 'pure maiden' or 'blessed maiden'. Although many people think of it as a variant of Rhiannon, it is a name in its own right.

Rhona, Rona (pronounced like 'ro + na')

No-one is certain when this name began to be used as a girl's name although it was certainly popular in Scotland during the nineteenth century. The spelling with 'h' has been influenced by 'Rhoda', which comes from Greek 'rose' or 'woman from Rhodes'. It is also possible that Rona is from Gaelic *rón*, meaning 'seal'. In Celtic tradition, women who lived in the sea often appeared as seals. Sometimes, the women would slough off their sealskin, revealing a beautiful woman. If a man managed to steal the skin, the sea woman would have to stay with him and be a dutiful wife. If she found the skin, however, she would put it on and go back to the sea. A number of Irish and Scottish families are said to be descended from seal women. Such people are often recognised by their webbed toes and their prowess as swimmers.

Rhonda (pronounced like 'ron + da')

Rhonda was popularised by the Hollywood actress, Rhonda Fleming. The name certainly looks Welsh and could be from *rhodd*, 'gift'. It may also have been influenced by the name of the Rhondda Valley, one of the best-known coal-mining regions in Wales.

Rhonwen (pronounced like 'hron + win')

Rhonwen is made up of *rhon* + *gwen*, meaning 'white lance', and it is probably linked with sunlight.
SEE: **Rowena**

Ríbh (pronounced like 'reeve')

Ríbh occurs in Lady Gregory's *Gods and Fighting Men*. In contemporary rural mythology, Ríbh is associated with a striped cat. If she allows you to stroke the cat, your good fortune is assured. The link between Ríbh and the striped cat may be due to folk etymology. The modern Irish word for 'stripe' is *riabh*.

Richael (pronounced like 'reech + hill')

Richael appears to be a traditional Gaelic name but it is virtually unused, having had its place taken by Rachel, which means 'ewe'. It is not clear what Richael means but the first part seems to relate to *rí*, 'king', and so it may mean 'royal child'. For parents who would like an unusual name, Richael seems to be tailor made.

Ríona, Rionach (pronounced like 'ree + in + a')

This lovely name comes from *ríon*, 'queen' and means 'like a queen'. It has been used as an abbreviated form of Caitriona but this is not what it comes from. Ríona has Our Lady as her special patron and so has a choice of feast days, including 25 March, 15 August and 8 September.

Riwanon (pronounced like 'ree + wan + on')
Riwanon is a Breton form of Rhiannon, which means 'moon goddess' or 'nymph'.
See: **Rhiannon**

Róisín (pronounced like 'rosh + een')
Róisín means 'little rose' and, as *roisín*, 'balm, comforter'. It has been used as a name for Ireland for five centuries and James Clarence Mangan translated a sixteenth-century poem, *Róisín Dubh*, as 'Dark Rosaleen'.

Rori, Ruarí (pronounced like 'ro + ree' and 'roo + ir + ee')
Rori comes from ruadhraí, meaning 'red-headed ruler'. It has begun to be used as a feminine form of Rory.

Rosmerta (pronounced like 'ross + mer + ta')
The meaning of Rosmerta's name is uncertain but it is said to mean 'supplier of food'. Certainly, there is a link with Gaelic ros, 'seed'. She was an early Celtic goddess, an earth-mother type. Rosmerta is certainly not widely used but it is a possible alternative to Rosemary.

Rowena (pronounced like 'ro + ween + na')
Many people who read Sir Walter Scott's novel *Ivanhoe* were captivated by the character and beauty of Lady Rowena. Scott may have made up the name, possibly as an anology with 'Rowan', from Gaelic *ruadhán*, meaning 'little red one', or it may be a Germanic name meaning 'fame and joy'. It is even possible that it is related to Rhonwen, 'white lance'.

Rozenn (pronounced like 'ro + zen')
Rozenn is a Breton name meaning 'rose'. Flower names have been popular for girls for at least two thousand years and they are popular again today. The rose is not only a beautiful flower, it has, for centuries, been associated with mysticism and the phrase 'rose without thorns' has been applied to Our Lady. Breton Rozenn is often thought to be in honour of St Rose of Lima.

Ryanne (pronounced like 'rye + an')
Ryanne has begun to be used in America as a female form of Ryan. It would thus mean 'little monarch'. It has the additional attraction of ending in 'Anne' and so parallels Joanne and Susanne.

Sadhbh, Sive (pronounced like 'sigh've')
Sadhbh's name means 'goodness,

sweetness'. It is related to modern Irish *sáimhe*, 'peacefulness, tranquillity'. She was transformed into a deer because she refused to marry Fionn MacCool, a man she did not love. However, when she was under Fionn's protection, she resumed her human form and Fionn married her. She was warned not to leave the safety of Fionn's household, but when she was pregnant her longing to walk in the woods overcame her good sense, and she was immediately transformed into a deer. Fionn mourned her loss for seven years but heard that there was a deer in the forest that his hounds would never hunt. He went to see for himself and found a female deer with a little boy. He recognised the child as his own and called him Oisín, which means 'little deer'.

SEE: **Oisín**

Saoirse (pronounced like 'seer + shih' or 'sare + shih')

Saoirse is a relatively new name in the Celtic tradition and is Irish for 'freedom'. It began to be used in the 1920s and gained an extra impulse in 1948, when the 'Irish Free State' became the 'Republic of Ireland'.

Saraid (pronounced like 'sor + id')

Saraid is attractive in both form and meaning, since it is related to *sár* and implies 'best, surpassing all'. The earliest record we have of the name is as the daughter of Conn of the Hundred Battles. Saraid, like her father, had second sight and the ability to travel to the 'other world' as an emissary. According to tradition, Saraid is the ancestor of the Gaelic- speaking people who settled in Scotland.

Scathach (pronounced like 'scah + hah')

Scathach was a Scottish warrior who may well have been a goddess. It is likely that the island of Skye is called after her. Her name is related to modern *scathach*, meaning 'shel- tered, shady'. Scathach was one of the greatest warriors of antiquity. So great was her fame that Cúchulainn went to Scotland to study martial arts under her.

Sceanbh (pronounced like 'scan + iv')

Sceanbh was the wife of a well-known traditional harper, called Craiftine, whose harp had the power to rouse warriors to feats of daring or to put them to sleep. Unfortunately, while Craiftine was playing his harp, Sceanbh was falling in love with Cormac, the son of Conchubhar! Sceanbh's name seems to be related to Gaelic *sceanbh*, 'a spike'.

Seirial

Seirial is related to Seirian and means 'bright, brightness'. It is occasionally thought to be a female form of Cyril, which is from a Greek name *kyrillos*, meaning 'lord', and so it carries the attractive meaning of 'bright lady'.

Seirian

Seirian is an attractive Welsh name,

meaning 'sparkling'. It is probably taken from *serennu*, 'sparkle', but may have been influenced by the Hebrew Sarah, meaning 'princess'.

Selma

Selma is probably from a Celtic word meaning 'fair, beautiful'. It is likely that it has been influenced by Anselm, a name that means 'God's helmet' and also, possibly, by Hebrew *shalom*, 'peace'.

Seonaid (pronounced like 'shone + aid'), Sinead, (pronounced like 'shin + aid'), Shaynee

These names are Gaelic forms of Jeannette or Janet, the first from Scotland and the second from Ireland. The Normans introduced the name as a feminine form of Jean, meaning 'John', a name of Hebrew origin implying 'God is gracious'. Sinead has been popularised by the actress Sinead Cusack and, more recently, by the singer Sinead O'Connor. Shaynee is sometimes used as a pet name.

Seosaimhín (pronounced like 'sho + siv + een')

Seosaimhín is the Irish form of Josephine, a name that became popular in France because of Napoleon's wife, the Empress Josephine. It is derived from Joseph, which means 'God shall add', a name that has been revered in Celtic communities since the introduction of Christianity.

Sererena (pronounced like 'ser + er + ena')

Sererena was a Cornish saint and the sister of Eulalia and Sapientia. It is possible that her name is a form of Latin *serena*, meaning 'calm'. She seems to have been martyred with St Ursula and 11,000 maidens.

SEE: **Eulalia**

Seve, Seva (pronounced like 'sev' and 'se + va')

These are Breton names that are probably related to Sadhbh and suggest 'peace, tranquillity'.

SEE: **Sadhbh**

Shanley (pronounced like 'shan + lee')

Shanley has not been widely used as a name, although its meaning is traditional. It probably comes from *sean + laoch*, 'old warrior', and implies 'daughter of the old warrior'. Occasionally, it is used as a female form of Seán, although the only link between the names is pronunciation.

Shanna, Shannagh, Shannan, Shannen, Shannon

These names are all probably derived from the River Shannon, which is related to *sean*, 'old', and means 'the old one'. (Interestingly, African Americans referred to the Mississippi as 'Ol' Man River'.) The names have probably been reinforced by the surname Shannaghan. It is also possible that Shanna has been influenced by Scottish Shona, which is another form of Joan.

Shaynee (pronounced like 'shay + nee')
SEE: **Seonaid**

Sheena, Síne (pronounced like 'shee + nih')
Sheena is an anglicised spelling of Síne, a Scots Gaelic form of 'Jeanne' or 'Jane'. All of these names are feminine forms of John, which means 'God is gracious'.
SEE: **Seonaid**

Sheila, Sheela, Sheelagh, Síle
Sheila is still widely used in Ireland but it was once so popular that the Australian slang term for 'woman' is 'sheila'. It is probable that Sheila is an Irish form of Cecilia, the patron saint of music, and so implies 'pure and musical'. It is possible, too, that the Irish name has been influenced by the Hebrew name 'Shelah', meaning 'longed-for'.

Shibley, Sibéal (pronounced like 'shib + lee' and 'shib + ale')
Shibley and Sibéal are forms of Isabel, which is a Spanish form of the Hebrew name Elisheba, meaning 'God is my oath'. Forms of Elizabeth have been popular throughout the Celtic world.
SEE: **Elspeth, Iseabeal**

Sian (pronounced like 'shan')
Sian is the Welsh equivalent of Gaelic Síne and they are both forms of 'Jeanne' or 'Jane', names that were popularised by the Normans and became even more widely used in the Celtic areas after the death of Jeanne d'Arc or Joan of Arc. St Joan's exploits in leading the French army are reminiscent of famous warrior queens, such as Boudicca or Madhbh.
SEE: **Sheena**

Sibeál,
SEE: **Iseabeal**

Síle
SEE: **Sheila**

Sinéad (pronounced like 'shin + aid')
This is an Irish form of Jeannette or Janet.
SEE: **Seonaid**

Siobhán, Shevaun, Chevonne, Siubhan, Siún (pronounced like 'shiv + awn' and 'shoo + win')
Siobhán is one of the best-known Gaelic names for girls, having been popularised outside Ireland by the actress Siobhán McKenna. Because English speakers found Siobhán hard to spell and pronounce, the name has bee anglicised as Shevaun and Shivaun, and frenchified as Chevonne. All of these names are versions of Susan, meaning 'lily', or Joan, meaning 'God is gracious'.

Sorcha (pronounced like 'sor + ha')
Sorcha is a traditional Gaelic name, *sorcha* meaning 'brightness, light'. (It thus parallels Welsh Seirial.) It is often regarded as the Irish equivalent of Sarah, a name that means 'princess' although there is no actual link between the names.

Tamsin, Tamasin, Tamzin

Tamsin is becoming increasingly popular. It is a modified form of Thomasina, and thus means 'female twin' and, although it was once popular throughout the British Isles, it was preserved only in Cornwall.

Tangwystl (pronounced like 'tang + wist + el')

For any parent looking for an exotic name for a child, Tangwystl is a clear favourite. It comes from Welsh and means 'pledge of peace' and is derived from *tagnefedd*, 'peace'.

Tara

Tara has become a girl's name in the recent past but it was originally the name of a royal prehistoric fort in Co. Meath dating back 4,000 years. Its meaning is not known but it possibly implies 'crag, hill' and is therefore related to modern 'tor' which means 'bulging hill' and is found in such placenames as Torquay in Devon and Torpoint in Cornwall. Many stories and songs are told about the splendours of Tara, where the high kings of Ireland were anointed, and many relate the sadness of its passing:

> The harp that once through
> Tara's halls, the soul of music fled
> Now hangs as mute on Tara's walls.

Tara has the additional attraction that it is also a Sanskrit word for 'star'.

Tearney, Teerney, Tierney

Tierney, however it is spelt, comes from *tighern*, 'lord', and means 'lordly, noble'. Like many girl's names, it may have been borrowed from the surname Tierney, which was originally a given name.

Tegan (pronounced like 'teg + an')

Tegan is a lovely Welsh name, related to *tegwch*, 'beauty', and meaning 'beautiful'. It is not, as yet, as popular as Megan, but there is no reason why it should not become so.

Tegwen, Tegwyn (pronounced like 'teg + win')

Tegwen is sometimes regarded as a more Welsh form of Tegan, but it seems to be a name in its own right, combining *tegwch*, 'beauty', and *gwyn*, 'fair, pure', and meaning 'beautiful and blessed'.

Tierney

SEE: **Tearney**

Trac(e)y, Trea, Treasa (pronounced like 'tray + see', 'tray + a' and 'trass + a')

These names are usually thought of as Irish forms of Teresa, the name of several saints, including the Carmelite nun, St Teresa of Avila, who used to hold conversations with God. However, there was an Irish noun *treise* that meant 'strength', a fact that helps to account for the popularity of Teresa. Teresa has many abreviations including Teezy, Teri, Terry and Tré.

Trina, Triona (pronounced like
'tree + (i)na')
Trina and Triona have become popular
recently. They are abbre- viations of
Catrina and Caitríona and so are
indirectly related to Hecate, a Greek
goddess of enchantment and to the
Greek word *katharos*, meaning 'pure'.

Tyrona, Tyronee (pronounced like
'tir + own + a' and 'tie + rone +
ee')
Both these names have been used in
America for the daughters of people
from Co. Tyrone. The county's name
tír + Eoghan means 'land of Eoghan'
and Eoghan means 'well born, noble'.
SEE: **Tyrone**

Early Celtic alphabets
did not make use of the letters
V, X, Y and Z and so we do not find
many examples of traditional
names beginning with
these letters.

Ula, Yula (pronounced like 'oo +
la' or 'yoo + la')
Ula is a Celtic name, probably from
ula, 'altar, tomb'. In parts of Ireland,
the name is associated with sealions,
who were thought to be fallen angels
that were so beautiful God took pity
on them and let them stay in the sea,
rather than forcing them into hell.

Ultána (pronounced like 'ool + taw
+ na')

Ultána has been used in Northern
Ireland as a female form of Ultán, 'an
Ulsterman'. There were several saints
called Ultán but, as far as we know,
none called Ultána. The name is
attractive, however, and seems likely
to grow in popularity.

Una , Úna, Oona, Oonagh
(pronounced like 'oo + na')
Una is often translated as Unity
because of the meaning of Latin *una*,
'one', but it appears to be an
indigenous Gaelic name possibly
associated with 'banshee'.

Valma, Valmai (pronounced like
'val + ma' and 'val + my')
Valma is said to be from *blodyn +
mai*, 'mayflower'. The name was
originally associated with the Blessed
Virgin Mary, to whom the month of
May was specially dedicated. It is not
always clear if one special flower is
meant. Often, it is said to be a lily of
the valley but others have suggested
that it refers to the cowslip.

Vevila, Vevan, Vevin
Vevila is said to include an
anglicised form of *Béibhinn* (pronounced 'Vevin' in the vocative),
meaning 'sweet, melodious lady' or
'fair lady'. It seems to have been
influenced also by Vivian, a Norman
name meaning 'alive'.
SEE: **Béibhinn**

Verity

Verity is not a Celtic name, but derived from Latin and meaning 'truth'. In Ireland, Fírinne, meaning 'truth' is sometimes used as a translation of Verity.

SEE: **Fírinne**

Vivanne, Vivian, Vivien, Vivienne

SEE: **Béibhinn**

Wallis

Wallis, like Wallace and Welsh, actually comes from an Anglo-Saxon word *wealh*, meaning 'foreigner'. The name is not often used as a girl's name but it gained some currency when Edward VIII abdicated in order to marry Wallis Simpson.

Wendy

Wendy deserves a mention in a dictionary because it is sometimes regarded as an abbreviation of Gwendoline. It seems, however, that the Scottish playwright, JM Barrie, coined it for one of the characters in *Peter Pan* because he had heard a child call another 'my fwendy' (my friend).

Wenn(a)

A St Wenna is found in Cornwall and may simply be a Cornish form of *gwen*, meaning 'blessed', and indeed one of Brychan's saintly daughters was Guen or Gwen.

SEE: **Gwen**

Winifred, Wynne

Winifred is a Germanic name meaning 'gracious friend' but it is often equated with the name of a seventh-century Welsh saint, *Gwenfrewi*, meaning 'fair + reconciliation' and with Wynne, from Welsh *gwen*, meaning 'fair', or *gwyn*, meaning 'blessed'.

SEE: **Gwen**

Yseult (pronounced like 'ee + solt')
Yseult is an alternative spelling of Isolde, Isolt or Iseult, probably meaning 'fair one'. The 'y' spelling goes back to a time when 'y' was used as an alternative spelling for 'I'. We still find a relic of this in a word like 'why'.

SEE: **Iseult**

BOYS' NAMES

Abloec (pronounced like 'ab + lock')
This is a Welsh and Cornish form of
the Viking name Havelock, which
means 'relic of God'.

Accalon (pronounced like 'ack +
al + on')
Accalon was from Brittany. His name
may be related to Welsh *achlod*,
'shame'. He was the lover of King
Arthur's sister Morgan le Fay and
planned to defeat Arthur by stealing
his sword, Excalibur. Accalon's plans
were frustrated by Merlin.

Adair, A'dair
This name comes from the same root
as Gaelic *doire*, meaning 'oak grove',
a place that was sacred to the Celts.
SEE: **Daren, Derry, Diarmaid**

**Adamnan, Ádhamhán,
Adomnan** (pronounced like 'a +
dawn + an' or 'ah + ow + nawn')
Adamnan may be a Gaelic form of
Adam or it may derive from a root
such as *adhain*, meaning 'kindle,
ignite'. It has also probably been
influenced by *ádhamhail*, 'lucky'.
The name has been recorded since
the seventh century AD, when St
Adamnan – or Adomnan or
Ádhamhán – (627-704) was abbot of
Iona. Adamnan was a writer and
scholar and is reputed to have been
the first person to have recorded a
sighting of Nessie, the Loch Ness
Monster.

Addis, Addison, Aidis (pronounced to rhyme with 'lad + iss'
or 'laid + iss')
This name is not as popular now as it
once was. It is related to *aodh*, 'flame,
fire'. The derived form Addison is
occasionally used as a given name in
Scotland.
SEE: **Aedh**

Adeon (pronounced like 'add +
eon')
Adeon was a Welsh prince, the
grandson of Caradoc. The name may
come from *adain*, 'wing', or it may be
related to Irish Aodh and mean
'bright fire'. According to legend,
Adeon's sister was Helena, the
mother of Constantine the Great, the
first Christian Emperor of Rome.
Helena was reputed to have found the
cross of Christ.

Adomnan
SEE: **Adamnan**

Adwen, Adwin (pronounced like
'add + win')
This name is almost certainly a
Cornish form of Adeon, meaning
either 'winged one' or 'bright fire'.

Aed(h), Aodh (pronounced like
'may')
It seems likely that Aed(h) was a god
of fire. The Gaelic word *aodh* means
'fire, flame'. It was also the name of a
sixth-century Irish saint and an
eighth-century high king. Yeats wrote
a poem around 1899, first entitled
'Aedh wishes for the cloths of
Heaven' and later changed to 'He
wishes' because few people knew how

to pronounce the god's name.
SEE: **Addis**

Ael (pronounced like 'ell' or 'ale')
The Breton name for the saint of the 5 May is Ael. There is also a feminine form *Aela*. Little is known about the original Ael but the name may be connected with rocks or a rampart – the Celts often built forts on high hills.

Aelhaeran, Alhaern, Alhern
(pronounced like 'al + (h)aran')
Aelhaern is from Welsh *ael*, meaning 'brow' + *haearn*, 'iron'. It is a strong name, suitable for a boy who might have a military career.

Aengus, Angus, Aonghus (pronounced like 'eng + iss' or 'ang + gus')
The first and third spellings are found mostly in Ireland, and Angus is the preferred Scottish form. Aengus, sometimes called Aengus Óg, was the god of love and poetry and his words were so beautiful to hear that bees and birds were attracted to them as if they were honey. The name probably means 'outstanding, exceptional'. Aengus fell in love with a beautiful girl he saw in a dream and endured many hardships in his struggle to find her. Yeats immortalised his search in 'The Song of Wandering Aengus'.

Afagdu
Afagdu's name probably means 'darkness, dark river'. The Welsh word for river is *afon* and black is *du*.

He was the son of Ceridwen. She tried to make her son as wise as Solomon.

Ahern, Aherne, Hearn, Hearne
This Irish name, which is related to *eachaidhe*, 'horse rider', is more frequently found as a surname now.

Aidan, Aod(h)án (pronounced to rhyme with 'aid + in' or 'aid + on')
It seems probable that these are both diminutive forms of Aedh and Aodh, both of which come from *aodh*, 'fire', but they have became names in their own right in honour of the seventh-century Irish saint who carried Christianity to Northumbria. In Irish folk traditions, Aidan is associated with strength of mind and courage of heart. The name may have meant 'little fire' originally and it is thought by some to herald stubbornness. There is a similar-sounding Breton name, Aodren, although this is normally given as equivalent to Adrian, originally referring to a man from Hadria, a town in Italy that gave its name to the Adriatic Sea.

Ailill (pronounced like 'all + yill')
Ailill was the king of Connaught and the husband of Madhbh (Maeve). His name seems to be linked to *áilleacht*, 'beauty', or *aileach*, 'rocky place'. There are many legends about Ailill and his wife, most of them involving competition. One of the most famous relates to the argument they had concerning whose herd of cattle was

greater. In order to win, Maeve needed the brown bull of Cooley – and she went to war to get it.

Aindrias
SEE: **Andrew**

Ainnle, Áinle (pronounced like 'awe + n + lya')
The meaning of Ainnle is uncertain but it may be related to *anghlonn*, 'fierce warrior'. The Irish legendary chieftain, Usna, had three sons, Ardán, Ainnle and Naoise. Naoise fell in love with Deirdre and all three brothers fled with her to Scotland to avoid the wrath of Conchubhar (Conor), the high king, who wanted to marry her.

Ainsley
SEE: **Ainslee**

Alair
Alair is a bright name coming from a Gaelic adjective meaning 'cheerful' and probably reinforced by *ealar*, 'salty'. In the past, salt was almost a synonym for 'vital, essential, valuable'.

It is still found in the English word *salary*, which originally meant 'money paid for the purchase of salt'.

Alan, Alain, Allan, Allen, Alun
It seems likely that this is a Breton name, related to *alp* meaning 'rock', although it is possible that it has been reinforced by a Gaelic meaning of 'cheerful and harmonious'. Certainly, one of William the Conqueror's allies was Alan, the Earl of Brittany, and

this form of the name is still used in Brittany rather than the French form Alain. Alan gave rise to the surnames Allan and Allen, both of which were subsequently used as first names.

The form with 'u' is almost exclusively Welsh and the character Alun of Dyded occurs in the Welsh story cycle, *Mabinogion*.

Alaisdair, Alaister, Alasdair, Alastair, Aleister, Alisder, Alister, Alusdur
There are numerous spellings of this Scots Gaelic form of Alexander, which probably comes from Greek *alexein* + *aner*, 'to defend' + 'man'. The Greek name implied 'warrior' and the exploits of Alexander the Great (356-323 BC) have ensured the popularity of this name worldwide. Scots also use several abbreviated forms of Alexander, namely Alec, Alick and Sandy.

Alban, Albanactus, Albin
These variants are thought to derive from the Latin *albanus*, 'white', although it is also possible that they are latinised forms of a Celtic word *alp*, meaning 'rock'. St Alban was martyred in England in AD 303 near the Hertfordshire town, St Albans. The preferred Breton form is Albin, although Aubin and Aube, meaning 'dawn', are also found. Scotland is known as *Alba* in Gaelic and the man's name could derive from a form of this, in the same way that Erin, a form of *Éire*, is used as a girl's name.

According to medieval legend, Brutus was the founder of Britain and Scotland was given to his third son, Albanactus.

Alec, Alick
SEE: **Alaisdair**

Aled, Aleid (pronounced like 'a + lid' with the main stress on 'a')
Aled has become popular in Wales. It may mean 'noble brow' but carries with it overtones of contemporary Welsh *alaeth*, 'sorrow'. The name has been given prominence by the singer Aled Jones.

Alef
Alef was a king of Cornwall and his name may be a form of the Viking name Olaf, meaning 'relic'. He planned to marry his daughter to a Pictish champion who was reputedly eight feet tall. As in many Celtic stories, the princess managed to find a champion and so married Sigtryg of Waterford, the son of the Danish king of Ireland.

Alaister
SEE: **Alaisdair**

Alhern
SEE: **Aelhaeran**

Alisder, Alister
SEE: **Alaisdair**

Allan, Allen
SEE: **Alan**

Almer
It is probable that Almer is the same name as Elmer and that they both derive from Anglo-Saxon *thol + mær*, meaning 'famously noble'. Almer seems to have been a Cornish nobleman in the early Middle Ages and the father of St Sitwell, although it is possible that both he and his daughter were Bretons.

Alroy
Alroy is from Gaelic and is a variant of *ruadh*, meaning 'red-head'. Its form has been influenced by Roy, which may be related to French *roi*, 'king'.

Alun
SEE: **Alan**

Aluster
SEE: **Alaisdair**

Amatheon (pronounced like 'a + math + eon')
In modern Welsh, *amaethyddiaeth* means 'agriculture'. Amatheon was a Welsh warrior who lived in the woods. It is possible that he was originally a fertility god. Certainly, his name is linked to farming.

Anarawd (pronounced like 'a + na + rod')
This Welsh name is related to *iawn*, 'very' + *huawdl*, 'eloquent', and means 'eloquent, beautifully spoken' and would be a gift for any child.

Andrew, Andrev, Aindrias
These are forms of Greek *Andreas*, meaning 'brave, manly, virile'. This name has been popular in all Celtic

communities since the introduction of Christianity. Andrew was, after all, the first apostle called by Jesus and he is the patron saint of Scotland. The English form Andrew is widely used, as are the diminutives Andie and Andy; the second form, Andrev, is preferred in Brittany; and the third, Aindrias, is found in Gaelic-speaking communities. The feminine forms Andrea and Andi are becoming popular.

Aneslis, Ainéislis (pronounced like 'an + ace + lish')
This unusual name is thought to be a Celtic form of Stanislaus, 'stand of glory'. A variety of it is found in the name of Standish O'Grady, author of *History of Ireland: Heroic Periods* (1860), who commented on the Irish penchant for turning history into poetry, so that 'the history of one generation became the poetry of the next'.

Aneurin (pronounced like 'an + eye + rin')
It is possible that Aneurin, which was the name of an early seventh-century Welsh poet, may be a form of Latin *Honorius*, meaning 'man of honour'. The poet Aneurin's work appears in a medieval manuscript and is, in part, a lament for the defeat of the North British – whose language is the same as Welsh – at the battle of Catterich in Yorkshire by the Anglo-Saxons. More recently, the name has been popularised in its full and its abbreviated form of Nye by Aneurin

Bevan (*ap* + *Evan*, 1897-1960), the British Labour Prime Minister who was born in Wales and renowned for his oratory.

Angus
SEE: **Aengus**

Angwyn
Welsh uses the adjective *gwyn*, meaning 'white, fair', in many of its names for both boys and girls. This one is the equivalent of 'very fair, very handsome'.
SEE: **Gwennin**

Annan
Annan occurs as a surname mainly in Scotland and seems to mean 'one who lives by the river'. The Celtic word for river can still be found in 'Avon' as in Stratford-upon-Avon and in Gaelic *abhann*, 'river'. The identical name Annan also occurs in Ghana and is given to the fourth son.

Aodh
SEE: **Aedh**

Aodhgagán (pronounced like 'ey + ga +gone')
This is a modified form of Aedh or Aodh and means 'little fire'. It has become a name in its own right and is frequently spelt Egan in Ireland and the Isle of Man, and Iagan in Scotland. It overlaps the Breton name Jagu or Jegu, although these are often thought to be Breton realisations of James in its French form, Jacques.
SEE: **Egan, Jago**

Aodán, Aodhán
SEE: **Aidan**

Aodren
SEE: **Aidan**

Aonghus
SEE: **Aengus**

Ardal, Ardghal (pronounced to rhyme with 'awe + r + gal')

This name is not very widely used although it may have a long Celtic heritage. It is possible that it comes from a combination of words *árd + geal* implying 'high courage'. It is also possible that it is a form of Art or Arthur since the use of 'l' instead of 'r' is found in other names, such as Hal and Harry or Molly and Mary. The 'l' instead of 'r' in Arthur was widely found in Brittany and Wales. It can be seen, for example, in the use of *Arthgallo* in the fourteenth-century *History of the Kings of Britain*, by Geoffrey of Monmouth.

Ardán (pronounced like 'are + dawn')

Ardán, which may mean 'tall fellow', is the name of one of the sons of Usna who accompanied Deirdre to Scotland so that she would not be forced to marry Conchubhar. It is not certain what the name means but it may be related to *árdánach* and imply 'high aspiration'.
SEE: **Ainnle, Conaire, Naoise, Usna**

Argyle (pronounced like 'are + guile')

Argyle is used mainly in Scotland. It is a placename meaning, appropriately enough, 'place of the Gaels'.

Armanz

This is the Breton form of French Armand, a name that is associated with courage and the bearing of arms and which probably means 'bearer of arms'. It may have been influenced by words beginning with *ar-*, meaning 'bear'. The bear was honoured by the Celts.

Art

An early Irish use of Art is found in the name of Cormac MacAirt, a legendary high king of Ireland. The name Art may come originally from Greek *arktourous*, 'keeper of bears', because the bear was sacred to all the Celts. It may also derive from an old Gaelic word *art*, 'stone'. It is also possible that it is the male equivalent of *Artio*, a Celtic bear goddess. Bears were found all over Europe when the Celts were the dominant tribe.
SEE: **Arthur, Artúr, Bernard**

Arthfael (pronounced like 'arth + file' or 'arth + fale')

This Welsh name is related to Arthur and is thought to mean 'strong as a bear'. It should be remembered that the Celts admired the bear for its endurance as well as its physical strength.

Arthur, Artúr (pronounced like 'art + oor'), Arzhul (pronounced like 'are + zool')

In the anglicised form Arthur, this name is known throughout the world because of the stories about King Arthur and the Knights of the Round Table. Like Art, the name may owe its origin to Greek *arktourous*, 'keeper of bears'. In the Celtic languages, however, it probably means 'bear' or 'strong as a bear'. King Arthur was a sixth-century Celtic chieftain who fought against the Saxons and whose exploits have been incorporated into the legends of chivalry. These have been recorded since the Middle Ages and were immortalised in poetry by Tennyson in *Idylls of the King*. Tradition has it that Arthur did not die but was spirited away to Avalon (or sometimes Avilion) and that he will return to rule again when justice and chivalry prevail. Another possible origin is *art*, 'bear' + '*úr*', 'fresh, pure'.

SEE: **Bernard**

Athol (pronounced like 'ath + el')
Athol is a placename in Scotland that may mean 'juniper tree' or it might be a reduced form of *áit*, 'place', + *Gael*, 'Gael'. It is the given name of the South African playwright, Athol Fugard.

Auley, Awley, Amhalghaidh
  (pronounced like 'awl + ee')
These are forms of a name that predates the Vikings in Ireland. No one is certain of its meaning although it may be related to modern Irish *amhailt*, 'a phantom', or *amhra*, 'a marvel'. Today, it is most frequently found in Macauley, as in the name of the American actor Macaulay Culkin.

Auliffe, Awlif, Amhlaoibh
  (pronouced like 'awl + if')
The Viking invaders spread over many parts of Europe from the seventh century and they left their mark on such placenames as Normandy (land of the North men), Swansea (swan's island) and Wicklow (Viking settlement). They also left some of their names behind. Olaf, for example, which means 'relic', gave rise to McAuliffe, meaning 'son of Olaf', and to other less obvious names such as McCausland, which is a modified form of Mac + Olaf + son, meaning 'son of Olaf's son'. The Vikings seem to have liked Niall and Oscar, which they took back to Scandinavia, where they are found in the first names Nils and Oskar and the surname Nilsen.

SEE: **Niall, Oscar**

Auryn (pronounced like 'aw + rin')
The Welsh, like the other Celts, probably took their word for 'gold' from Latin. The noun *aur* means 'gold' and Auryn implies 'golden one'. The name could thus be applied to a boy with golden hair or to a child that has been longed for. Ireland was rich in gold and so the Celts also had a word for it: *ór*.

Austell (pronounced like 'ows' + tell' or 'awes' + tell')
This name occurs in the medieval

Life of St Mewan which was written in Brittany. Austell was the Cornish godson of Mewan and he is honoured in both the Cornish placename St Austell and the Welsh placename Llanawstl, meaning 'church of Austell'.

Avallach

Avallach was the king of Avalon, which seems to come from *afal* 'apple' + *ynys*, 'island'. King Arthur was taken to Avallach's kingdom to be healed of his wounds and to stay until the time of his second coming, when peace and justice would prevail.

Balfour

It may be a folk etymology, but it is said that Balfour comes from a Gaelic greeting meaning *Bail ó Dhia ar an fhoghmar*, 'The blessings of God on the harvest'. The name was popularised by R.L. Stevenson's *David Balfour*, a sequel to *Kidnapped*.

Balor

Balor was a king of Ireland. His name may be related to *balbh*, 'dumbfounded'. Balor lost one of his eyes by spying on the Druids in the hope of discovering the secret of their wisdom.

Banadel, Benedalor

Banadel was a medieval Welsh king who was the father-in-law of St Brechanus, or Brecon, who gave his name to the Brecon region, now part of Powys. The name seems to be derived from *ban* 'peak' + *addoll*, 'worship' and imply 'holy hill'.
SEE: **Brecon**

Banier

Banier was one of the Knights of the Round Table. His name seems to be related to Welsh *ban*, meaning 'peak', and it has been reinforced by *baner*, 'flag'.

Banning

This name comes from a blend of *bán*, 'white', + *finn*, 'fair, golden' and suggests 'very fair child'. The '-ing' ending is by analogy with such surnames as Canning.

Banquo (pronounced like 'bank + wo')

Banquo's name is familiar to anyone who has read Shakespeare's *Macbeth*, in which the ghost of murdered Banquo returns to haunt the king. Banquo, like Banning, derives from *bán* which means 'white, fair' and possibly from '*bán chú*', 'white hound'.

Bard, Baird

The word *bard* or *bárd* occurs in the Celtic languages with the meaning of 'poet'. A modified form, Baird, is a popular surname in Scotland and has begun to be used as a given name.

Barinthus

Barinthus is a Welsh form of Barnabas, a Hebrew name meaning 'son of consolation'. Barinthus is also the latinised form of *Barr-fhind* or *Barr Fhionn*, 'white top'.

SEE: **Barnaby, Fionnbharr (Finbarr)**

Barnaby, Barnaib, Barney

This name comes ultimately from the Hebrew name Barnabas, meaning 'son of consolation'. It has become popular over the last decade. The form Barney is sometimes used as a modified form of Bernard. The Welsh Barinthus, whose name may be a variant, helped Arthur to find Avalon.

Barra, Barris, Barry, Baz, Bazza, Bearach

These all seem to be related and probably come from *bearach*, meaning 'spear' and implying 'warrior'. The Barry form is used both as a given name and a surname, and the 'z' forms are found mostly in Australia and in the southeast of England – Barry is the English form of Fionnbharr. The name Barry has spread widely outside Celtic communities and is occasionally used as a reduced form of Bartholomew. Finbar means 'fair-headed Barry'. The name Barris means 'Barry's son'.

SEE: **Finbarr**

Bartley

This is an Irish form of the Hebrew name Bartholemew, 'son of Talmai'.

SEE: **Parthalán**

Baruch

It is not certain whether Baruch is another form of *bearach*, 'spear', or whether it is a name in its own right. This form of the name is identical to the Hebrew Baruch who was a disciple of Jeremiah and who is reputed to have written the Apocrypha. The Hebrew Baruch means 'blessed'.

SEE: **Barra**

Bastian

This is the Breton form of Sebastian, a name that meant 'man from Sebasta', a place in Asia Minor. Sebastian was one of the most popular of saints and was frequently depicted in art. He is reputed to have been a soldier who was martyred for his faith in 303. He is usually portrayed as a young man pierced with many arrows. According to legend, he survived the arrows but infuriated the Emperor Diocletian by continuing to proclaim Christianity. He was condemned to be beaten to death.

Baudwin

Baudwin is a French form of Baldwin, meaning 'brave or bold friend'. Baudwin was a Breton Knight of the Round Table. He was renowned for his skill as a doctor and also for his piety. When Arthur was defeated, Baudwin became a hermit and dedicated himself to the service of God.

Baz, Bazza

SEE: **Barra**

Beacán, Beagán, Beagen (pronounced like 'beg + awn' or 'bug + awn')

This name probably originated as a nickname, deriving from *beagán*, meaning 'little one', but it was the given name of a sixth-century Irish saint.

Bearach
SEE: **Barra**

Bedivere, Bedwyr, Belvedere

Bedivere was a Knight of the Round Table who remained loyal to Arthur. His name may be related to Welsh words *bad + gwr*, 'boatman', or *beddargraff*, 'epitaph', or it may come from French and mean 'good to look at, handsome'. Bedivere took the dying king to the lake and was asked to throw the sword, Excalibur, into the water. Twice, he failed to follow Arthur's instructions, but on the third occasion he threw the sword into the middle of the lake. An arm appeared waving the sword and a boat came to take Arthur to Avalon.

Beineón (pronounced like 'ben + yone'), Benan, Benead, Benignus, Benniget

All of these names derive from Latin adjectives meaning 'benign, blessed'. The first three have been used in Ireland, the last two in Brittany. The pet names Ben and Benny are more widely used and are often thought to derive from Benjamin, which may mean 'son of my sorrow' in Hebrew.

Bernard, Bernez

Bernard was popularised by the Normans and may have appealed to the Celts because it meant 'brave, hardy bear'. The bear was admired by the Celts for its strength and courage. The forms Bernie, Barnie and Barney are used as diminutives, as is Barn in Australia. Bernez occurs in Brittany.
SEE: **Art, Arthur**

Berwin, Brewin, Breward, Branwalader

Berwin was an early saint who may have been either Welsh or Cornish. He certainly seems to have been buried in Cornwall and his name has been spelt in a variety of ways. His name seems to be associated with *bendith*, meaning 'blessing'.

Bevan, Bevin (pronounced like 'bev + an')

This name is an anglicised form of *ap + Evan*, 'son of God's gracious gift'.
SEE: **Evan**

Bladud (pronounced like 'blad + oodh')

Bladud was a Celtic king whose name probably comes from *blaidd*, meaning 'wolf'. He is reputed to have built Bath, *Caer B(l)adud*, 'Bladud's fort'.

Blair

The name Blair occurs mainly in Scotland as both a first name and a surname. It seems to come from *blár*, meaning 'plain' and suggesting 'one from the plains'.

Blaise, Bleiz

There are at least two Blaises in Celtic tradition: the secular and the saintly. The former was a magician who trained Merlin and who had the gift of second sight. The name may be related to *blas*, 'taste, flavour', and this may partly account for the tradition that Blaise can heal sore throats. A Saint Blaise o Blasins was a devout doctor who was martyred. He was renowned for his kindness to animals, and can be seen in this capacity as a precursor of St Francis of Assisi. The form Bleiz is found in Brittany and there is a town called St Blazey in Cornwall. The French philosopher, Pascal, had Blaise as his first name.

Bowen

This name is probably a modification of Welsh *ap* + Owen, 'son of the noble warrior'.

SEE: **Eoghan, Owain**

Bowie (pronounced like 'bough + ee')

This name is perhaps most closely associated with the 'Bowie knife'. It derives from Gaelic *buidhe*, meaning 'yellow', and was probably given originally as a nickname to a golden-haired person.

Boyd, Boyden

Boyd, like Bowie, derives from *buidhe* and refers to yellow-gold. It is now most frequently used as a surname. Boyden may be a diminutive of Boyd or, more likely, it may come from *buaidh* meaning 'victory' and suggesting 'herald of victory'.

SEE: **Bowie**

Bradán, Braden (pronounced like 'brad + awn' and 'bray + den')

Both these forms, as first names and as surnames, seem to come from the Gaelic word *bradán*, meaning 'salmon'. There are numerous examples in Celtic literature of people being transformed into animals, birds, fish and insects.

SEE: **Beara, Blodeuwedd, Etain, Oisín**

Bradie, Brady

These names derive from the Irish surname, which may come from *bradán*, 'salmon', or they may have been from English 'broad + ey', meaning 'island'. A similar ending is found in Swansea, 'swan's island'.

Bran

Bran is an old Celtic word *bran(n)*, meaning 'raven', a bird that was sacred to all the Celts and may have been a harbinger of death. The name has been held by a Welsh giant-like god who possessed a liquid that could restore life (whiskey = the water of life); by an Irish navigator who found an island inhabited only by women; and by Fionn MacCool's wolfhound. Names like Brannagan and Brannigan are diminutives of Bran.

SEE: **Banba**

Brandan, Brandon

SEE: **Brendan**

Brandubh (pronounced like 'bran + doo')

Brandubh comes from *bran + dubh*

and means 'black raven'. It is the name of a seventh-century king of Leinster and also the name of a chess-like game sometimes played by Celts in trials of wit.

Brannoc, Brannock (both pronounced like 'bran + nock'), Brynach

It seems that Brannoc's name is related to *bran* + *ieuanc*, meaning 'young raven'. Brannoc came from the royal house of Calabria in Italy but worked as a priest in sixth-century Cornwall. He is known as Brannoc in Cornwall, and his name is given as Brynach in Wales. He is particularly associated with Braunton (Brannoc's town) in England and Llanfrynach (Brynach's church) in Wales. Some of the stories of his miracles suggest that he may have been linked with a Celtic god or magician. He could restore the life of an animal that had been killed and pluck loaves of bread from oak trees. There is also an early Breton saint, Branwalader, who may be the same person. Because of the tendency to spell names in a variety of ways, it is not always possible to know whether we are dealing with one person or several.

Branwell

Branwell is a Cornish name meaning 'raven's well'. Patrick Brontë, father of the famous Brontë sisters, married a Cornish woman whose surname was Branwell and called his son Patrick Branwell Brontë.

Branwalader
SEE: **Berwin, Brannoc**

Brastias

Brastias was a Knight of the Round Table who seems to have come from Cornwall. He was renowned for his loyalty to Arthur. His name may derive from French *bras*, 'arm', and mean 'well-built, strong and brave'.

Breandán
SEE: **Brendan**

Brassal, Breasal, Breasil

There are many forms of this name, which are related to Irish *breaslann*, 'king's court, palace', and the name was held by various gods and kings in early Ireland.

Brecon, Bregon, Brochan, Brychan (pronounced like 'breck + on', 'breg + on', 'broch + hon' and 'brooh + hin')

It it possible that these names are all related although they have been given to many different men. It is similar to the Welsh placename, Brecon, and probably comes from the Welsh word *brenin*, 'king'. Bregon or Brecon was like Abraham, in that he left his original home and established a great dynasty. Bregon was the father of all the Milesians, the people who were thought to be the first Celts in Ireland. Another holder of this name, sometimes spelt Bregon or Brychan, was a Welsh king whose claim to fame was that he had 12 sons and 12 daughters, each of whom became a saint. The Breton name, Brochan, seems to be related and they may all come from the word for badger, *broc*, an animal that was important to the Celts. Relics of this importance may be seen in the Highland tradition of using badger fur on sporrans.

Brendan, Brandan, Brandon, Breandán

Versions of this name are found in all of the Celtic regions and Brittany celebrates his feast day on 16 May. There are at least 16 saints who bear this name, but many of the legends are about Brendan the Navigator. He seems to have been born in Kerry, although his name may come from a Welsh word *brenin*, meaning 'king'. Tradition has it that he set sail in a small boat with a group of monks in the early sixth century and was the first European to visit America. It has been suggested that episodes in Jonathan Swift's *Gulliver's Travels* owe their origin to some of the stories associated with Brendan and Maeldún.

SEE: **Maeldún**

Brett, Bret

Brett is becoming increasingly popular. It is probably a form of *Breiz*, 'Brittany', suggesting 'native of Brittany' but it might also come from *ap* + Rhett, 'son of the ardent one'.

SEE: **Reece**

Briac, Briag, Briagenn (pronounced like 'bree + ack')

These are Breton forms of Brian, meaning 'noble, strong'.

SEE: **Brian**

Brian, Briant, Brion, Bryan

This name has become popular all over the world and seems to come from *brígh*, meaning 'noble, strong, virtuous'. Two of the most illustrious Brians are found in Ireland. The first was a warrior who killed the father of an Irish god, Lugh of the Long Arm, and was forced to fulfil a number of almost impossible tasks in order to appease Lugh. Brian and his brothers achieved all that Lugh demanded but died in the fulfilment of the last task. There are many parallels between this pre-Christian Brian and the High King, Brian Boru, who defeated the Vikings at the Battle of Clontarf, in 1014, but died of wounds received in the battle.

SEE: **Llew, Lugh**

Brice, Bryce

These are both forms of Welsh *ap* + *rhys*, 'son of the ardent one'. It is also possible that the name is from an older Celtic adjective meaning 'alert'.

Bricriú (pronounced like 'brick + roo')

Bricriú is sometimes referred to as 'Bricriú of the Bitter Tongue' because he was skilled at starting rows. He lived during the reign of Conchubhar and started a famous row between warriors and their wives about who was the greatest champion. His name seems to come from *brice*, 'speckled, freckled'.

Broc, Brock

The badger or *broc* was sacred to the Celts, so accounting for the survival of the name not only in the Celtic languages but in dialects of English and in names such as Brock and Brocklehurst. The name is less popular in Ireland than in other parts of the world because there is an Irish word *broc* that means 'refuse, left-overs'.

Brochan

SEE: **Brecon, Broc**

Brodie, Brody

Brodie comes from Scots Gaelic *brothaigh*, 'rampart'. It is possible that this name goes back to Pictish. The Clan Brodie has 'Unite' as its motto.

Bruce

There was a period when Bruce was one of the most popular names in Australia. Its original meaning is probably 'Brix, France' or 'Bruges, Belgium'. Bruce became inextricably linked to Scotland because of Robert the Bruce, who became King of Scotland in 1306 and defeated the English at Bannockburn in 1314.

Brychan

SEE: **Brecon**

Bryn

The Welsh name Bryn, meaning 'hill', may have contributed to the popularity of Brian. Bryn is certainly popular in Wales and Cornwall, and the existence of the Ivy League university Bryn Mawr (big hill) has encouraged its use in the United States.

Brynach (pronounced like 'brin + ock')

SEE: **Brannoc**

Buadhach (pronounced like 'boo + ock')

This attractive name comes from *buadhach*, meaning 'victorious', and would make an excellent alternative to Victor.

Buchanan

This Scottish clan name comes from Gaelic *both* + *chanain*, meaning 'house for the canon'. The Buchanans held land in the vicinity of Loch Lomond.

Budoc, Budog (pronounced like 'boo + dock'), Buddug

Budoc or Budog was a saint whose story indicates the closeness of the Celtic communities in the past. His mother is said to have been Azenor, a Breton princess. He was born in a barrel, brought up in Ireland, worked in Wales and is the patron saint of Cornwall. There is no record of his having visited Scotland or the Isle of Man. His name may be a form of *buadhach*, meaning 'victorious'. This name is the modern equivalent of Boudicca or Boadicea. Buddug is the Welsh version.

C

Cabhán, Cavan (pronounced like 'kav + an')

Although this Gaelic name comes from *cabhán*, meaning 'grassy hill or hollow', it is more frequently associated with the Ulster county of Cavan than with a child's name. It is occasionally used, and has influenced the spelling of 'Kevan'.
SEE: **Caoimhghín**

Caddell

This is used more frequently as a surname but it was originally a form of *cathal*, a first name meaning 'brave, spirited in battle'.

Caddock (pronounced like 'cad + dock'), **Cado, Cadoc, Cadog, Kadec, Kadeg**

Caddock probably comes from *cathach*, meaning 'brave in battle'. The life of St Cadoc, occasionally Cadog, was written in Wales in the twelfth century. Cadoc was a prince, the son of Gwynllyh and Gwladys. He became abbot of Llancarfan but travelled widely in Cornwall, Ireland, Scotland and Brittany, as well as making pilgrimages to Rome and Jerusalem. He is said to have known King Arthur. Cadoc was extremely popular in both Wales and Cornwall in the Middle Ages. Over 30 churches were dedicated to him and his well in Cornwall was visited by pilgrims. He seems also to have had followers in Brittany, where the variants Cado, Cadoc, Kadec and Kadeg are still used and where the meaning is sometimes related to *cadeau*, 'present, gift'.

Cadeyrn (pronounced like 'cad + er + in')

This Welsh name derives from *cad*, 'battle', and *cadarn*, 'strong', and suggests 'lord of battle'.

Cado, Cadoc, Cadog
SEE: **Caddock**

Cadogan (pronounced like 'cad + dug + gan' or 'kay + doo + gawn')

The name Cadogan occurs in *Some Experiences of an Irish R.M.*, a series of stories by Somerville and Ross. It comes from the Celtic words for 'battle'. Welsh has *cad* and Gaelic *cath* and it suggests 'one strong in battle'. It is also possible that Cadogan comes from *catachán*, a nickname meaning 'curly-headed'.

Cadwallader (pronounced like 'cad + wol +a + der')

This mouth-filling Welsh name probably comes from *cad*, 'battle' + *arweinyddiaeth*, 'leadership', and suggests 'leader in battle'.

Cahal, Cathal (pronounced like 'ka + hal')

This traditional Gaelic name comes from *cathal* and means 'powerful in battle'. It has various spellings including, occasionally, Kathal. Although it is not related to Charles or Carolus, it is often translated into English as 'Charles'.

Cahir, Cathaoir (pronounced like 'ka + here')

This name comes from *cathair*, 'guard'. It is related to Cathal and was the name of a High King of Ireland. The name is most common among the O'Doherty family and has become popular in both spellings but also, occasionally, as Caheer.

Cai, Kai, Kaie, Kay, Kaye, Ke, Quay (pronounced like 'kay')

This is the name of King Arthur's foster brother. The name is spelt in a variety of ways and may be related to a Welsh word, *cad*, for 'battle', or it may be a form of the Latin name Gaius. Sir Kay occurs in different guises in many of the Arthurian tales, often admired and feared because of his sharp wit. One story tells of his courage and bravery in rescuing Mabon, who had been stolen from his mother when he was three days old. The name is still found in Brittany, where it occurs in the forms Ke, Kaie and Quay.

Cáirbre, Cairpre (pronounced like 'car + brih' or 'car + ber + ry')

The meaning of this name is uncertain, although it may be related to the Gaelic adjective *cairbreach*, meaning 'rugged', or come from *cairbre*, 'charioteer'. Cáirbre is common as a surname, written as Carbery, Carberry and Carbury. There are many Cáirbres in Irish tradition, including a poet, a saint, a prince and a warrior.

Calatin

Calatin was an Irish warrior. His name may be related to *callshaoth*, meaning 'trial, difficulty'. He was killed in battle by Cúchulainn but avenged by his daughters. They made Cúchulainn see a phantom army and were thus instrumental in his death.

Caley

This Gaelic name comes from *caol*, 'slender', and would thus be equally appropriate for a girl.

Calhoun, Calquhoun, Colquhoun (pronounced like 'ca + hoon')

This Scottish name probably comes from Gaelic *Mac a' Chombaich*, 'son of the forester'. The motto for anyone of this name is *Si je puis*, 'If I am able to'.

Calidore

Calidore was reputed to be one of the gentlest and at the same time one of the most courageous of King Arthur's knights. The meaning of his name is uncertain but it may come from French *caillou d'or* and imply 'golden stone'.

Callum, Calum

Callum, with either a single or double 'l', is a Scottish form of Colm and comes from Latin *columba*, meaning 'dove'. The symbol of the dove represented the Holy Ghost and it also represented the qualities of gentleness and purity. The best-known saint was the sixth-century Columba, who was born in Ireland but established the monastic settlement on Iona and is credited with having converted large parts of Scotland and the north of England to Christianity.

SEE: **Colm**

Calquhoun
SEE: **Calhoun**

Camber
According to legend, Britain was founded by the Roman, Brutus. Camber was the son of Brutus and founder of Wales, *Cymru*.

Camden
Camden probably comes from *cam + dean*, meaning 'winding valley'. It is a placename that has been transferred to people as both a given name and a surname.

Cameron
The Camerons are a Highland clan renowned for their courage and resourcefulness. The name, which is used both as a surname and a given name, seems to come from the nickname meaning 'crooked nose', from *cam*, 'crooked', and *srón*, 'nose'. The Cameron motto is in Gaelic, *Aonaibh ri cheile*, 'Unite'.

SEE: **Camryn**

Campbell
Campbell is most frequently used as a Scottish surname. Like Cameron, it is a clan name, but its meaning is hotly debated – especially by the Campbells. Some people argue that it

comes from *cam*, 'crooked' + *éul*, 'mouth'; others point to the 'p' in the name and claim that it comes from Latin *de campo bello*, 'concerning the field of battle'. Either way, the name is attractive and is increasingly being given as a first name. In Gaelic Scotland it is always written Cambeulach.

Canank, Cannock, Cynog, Kinnock
Like a lot of early saints, this one has different names in different places. He is Canank, Canack and Kanack in Cornwall and Cynog in Wales. The name seems to come from *cynnig*, meaning 'offer'.

Canice, Coinneach (pronounced like 'can + iss' and 'kin + noch')
Canice seems to be from Gaelic *coinneach*, 'attractive person', and so it could be used for either a girl or a boy. Its association with males is due to the fact that a sixth-century Irish missionary priest used the name. Coinneach is also the founder of Cill Choinnigh (Kilkenny), whose cathedral is St Canice's. Coinneach was better known in Britain by his Latin name Canicus or by Kenneth in Scotland.

SEE: **Kenneth**

Caoilte (pronounced like 'keel + che')
It is not certain what Caoilte's name means, although it may be linked to *caol*, 'slender', or *caoidheamhail*, 'courteous'. Caoilte was a member of

the Fianna and renowned as its fastest runner. When Fionn MacCool was held hostage, Caoilte was able to run throughout the known world until he had brought Fionn's captors two wild animals of each species.

Caoimhghín, Caoimhín

(pronounced like 'cave + een' and 'keev + een'), **Cavin, Kevan, Kevin**

This name is found throughout the world as well as in every Celtic community. It comes from *caomh*, 'beautiful, gentle', and means 'beautiful at birth' or 'handsomely born'. St Kevin was a seventh-century monk who lived at Glendalough and was renowned throughout the Celtic world. The forms Coemgen, Gavin and Kevin are found in Brittany; at least one parish was dedicated to St Keverne in Cornwall; and Kevin is favoured in Scotland, Wales and the Isle of Man.

SEE: **Cavan, Gavin**

Caradec, Caradeg, Caradoc, Caradog

In the first century, the Celtic chieftain Caractacus or Caratacus rebelled against the Romans in Britain. He was defeated, but behaved with such courage that he is mentioned by Tacitus in his Histories. The name comes from Welsh *car*, meaning 'beloved', and it occurs as Caradoc or Caradog in Wales and as Caradec or Caradeg in Brittany. The Irish adjective *caradach*, 'friendly', may also have

contributed to the popularity of the name. The Irish form Cárthach is anglicised as Carthage.

Carannog (pronounced like 'ka + ran + ogue'), **Carantec, Carantoc, Carantog, Karantoc, Karanteg**

Carannog or Carantoc was a Welsh saint who was, it appears, a friend of St Patrick with whom he worked in Ireland and from whom he took a new name, *cearnach*, meaning 'victorious'. Carannog returned to Wales and Cornwall and is renowned for having saved King Arthur from a vicious serpent, a talent he may have picked up from his mentor, Patrick, who banished snakes from Ireland. The name is still found in Brittany in the forms Carantec and Karanteg.

Carey, Cary (pronounced like 'care + ee')

The name of the river Cary in Somerset is of Celtic origin, possibly *car*, meaning 'well loved', or perhaps more likely 'stony' or 'castle dweller'. The name was adopted as a surname by some Somerset people and as a first name by the filmstar Archie Leach, better known as Cary Grant. It is also spelt Carey. A second source of this name is the Irish surname Carey or Cary. This name may come from the Gaelic word *ciar*, meaning 'dark'. The third source may be the Welsh word *caer*, for 'fort, castle', found in such placenames as Caernarvon.

C

Carl
SEE: **Carroll**

Carlin, Carling
It is possible that this name comes from English *carling*, meaning 'little churl', but it would certainly have been reinforced in Celtic communities by its associated meaning of *cearbhall + ín*, 'little champion'.

Carney, Cearnaigh, Cearney, Kearney
This Irish name comes from *ceárnach*, 'victorious', and implies 'victorious warrior'.

Carollan
This is a diminutive of Carroll and means 'little champion'.
SEE: **Carroll**

Carrick, Carrig
These names and similar forms derive from the Gaelic word *carraig* for 'rock'. They are attractive but are less widely used than the variant Craig.
SEE: **Craig**

Carroll, Cearúil, Cearbhall, Carl, Karl
These are versions of an ancient name *cearbhall*, probably meaning 'fierce warrior'. They are found most frequently as surnames and Carroll is probably avoided as a boy's name because it sounds like Carol, Carl often being preferred. It is an interesting fact that, although the surnames of Celts were often originally men's given names, they are equally likely to be given to girls, especially if they end in '-y'.

Carvey
Carvey occurs mainly as a surname. It may come from *cairbthe*, 'naval', or *cearbhaidhe*, meaning 'like an elk, athletic'.

Casey
This name is growing in popularity, particularly in America. The legendary Casey Jones was an engine driver who gave his life to save the passengers on his train. The Irish surname Casey probably comes from *cathasach* and means 'war vigilant'.

Cass(idy)
The Irish surname Cassidy is of uncertain meaning, although it may be from *cas*, 'curly haired'. It is attractive in full, or shortened to Cass. There is a folk tradition that a Cassidy was always the doctor for the O'Neill clan.

Caswallawn (pronounced like 'cas + wa + hlawn')
The meaning of Caswallawn is not clear. It may be related to *caswir*, 'truth'. Caswallawn was a legendary Welsh prince who was in love with the beautiful Ffleur, or Fflur. She was carried off by a powerful enemy and Caswallawn sought her even as far as Rome. Caswallawn is like Aengus in being unable to rest without the woman on whom he has set his heart.

Cathbad, Cuthbert (pronounced like 'kah + bud')
Cathbad's name seems to be related

to *cath*, 'battle'. He was a druid priest renowned for his prophecies. He foretold, for example, that a boy would take up arms and be among the greatest warriors of all time. He added, however, that the hero's life would be short. Cúchulainn fulfilled this prophecy. He also prophesied the pain and destruction that would result from Conchubhar's passion for Deirdre.

Cathmore

This is an unusual Irish name, which comes from *cath + mór*, meaning 'great battle' and implying 'great warrior'.

Cavan, Cavin

This can be a regional pronunciation for Kevin and thus be related to *caoimhneas*, meaning 'gentleness'. It is also possible that it is the placename, as in County Cavan.
SEE: **Caoimhghín**

Cearbhall
SEE: **Carroll**

Cearnaig, Cearney
SEE: **Carney**

Cearúil
SEE: **Carroll**

Cecil

Cecil comes ultimately from an old Welsh name *seissylt*, meaning 'sixth', that was given to a sixth child. Later, it became the surname of a family that rose to power under Elizabeth I. Later still, it became popular as a first name and was the given name of a world-famous American film director Cecil B(lount) De Mille.

Cedric

The name Cedric seems to have been used first by Sir Walter Scott in his novel *Ivanhoe*. It may be of Celtic origin, related to *céadrith*, and mean 'first choice', or it may simply have been made up.

Celtchair (pronounced like 'kelt + hair')

Celtchair was an Irish warrior who lived at the time of Cúchulainn. His name may be related to *cealtair*, meaning 'mask', or *ceilt*, 'concealment'. Celtchair found out that his wife had a lover and he killed him in anger, in the presence of Concubhar and Cúchulainn, who were playing a game like chess. Some of the blood fell on the board and Celtchair had to be punished for this breach of etiquette.

Ceran
SEE: **Ciarán**

Cerwyn

This Welsh name from *car + gwyn* means 'fair love' and would be appropriate for either a girl or a boy.

Christie, Críostaí

Christopher means 'bearer of Christ' and the diminutive Christie is popular in Ireland and Scotland. The preference of Christie over Chris may be accounted for by the fact that *Críostaí* is the Gaelic word for Christian.

Cane, Cian, Kane, Kean, Keane

These names possibly come from different sources but they have reinforced each other. Cian probably comes from Gaelic *cian*, meaning 'ancient', and it is used for both boys and girls, especially in the form of Kean. There is a female Carribean linguist, for example, called Kean Gibson. The Gaelic name *Cathán*, meaning 'warrior', gave rise to the surnames Kane and O'Kane which, in their turn, encouraged Cane and Kane as given names.

SEE: **Kean**

Ciarán (pronounced like 'kee + er + awn' or 'kee + rin'), Kieran, Kieron, Keiran, Ceran, Queran

These names are the most frequently used variants of Gaelic *Ciarán*, meaning 'little dark one'. The name has been popular for over 1,500 years and at least 26 saints have borne it. One of the best known was the abbot of Clonmacnoise, and his feast day is still celebrated in Brittany on 5 March.

Cillian, Killian

This name may come from *cill*, 'church', and mean 'associated with the church', or *ciall*, 'good sense'. It is popular in Ireland but also in both France and Germany, where two Irish Cillians worked as missionaries. The forms Kilian and Kilien are preferred in Brittany.

Clancy

Unlikely as it seems, this name comes from *flann* + *cath*, meaning 'red(headed) warrior'. It has been adopted as a first name, especially in America, from the surname Clancy, which came from MacFhlannchaidh, 'son of the red warrior'.

Clearie, Cleary

The Irish surname Clearie or Cleary is occasionally used as a given name. It probably comes from Gaelic *cliaraí*, meaning 'minstrel, scholar'.

Cledwin

This Welsh name is one of several that come from *cledd*, meaning 'sword'. This name is roughly the equivalent of 'blessed sword'.

Clooney, Cluny

Clooney is Gaelic and may come from *cluain*, meaning 'grassy meadow'. It might be an appropriate name for a farmer. There is a possibility that the name comes from a similar-sounding Irish noun meaning 'flattery', so a Clooney would be one who could 'while the birds off the bushes' with the sweetness of his speech.

Clyde

Clyde is best known as a river in Scotland but it is occasionally used as a first name. It may mean 'warm' as in Welsh *clyd*, 'snug', or perhaps it has the more appropriate meaning of 'powerful enough to be heard from a distance'.

Coinneach

SEE: **Canice**

Colin, Coll, Collen, Cul(l)an, Cullen, Coilín

There are a number of explanations for these names. Coll(a), from *coll*, meaning 'high, chieftain', has been used in Scotland and Ireland and was reinforced by the use of Col as a medieval diminutive of the Greek form of Nicholas, meaning 'people's victory'. The Gaelic words *caileán* and *coileán*, meaning 'cub, young one', may well have resulted in the popularity of Colin and Cullen as first names.

SEE: **Cúchulainn, Cullan**

Colm, Colum, Colmcille, Columb, Columba, Coulm, Colman, Kolman

All these are variants of Latin *columba*, meaning 'dove'. The dove symbolised peace, purity and the Holy Ghost and was used by churchmen in all areas of the Celtic world. There are over 30 saints whose name has been a form of Latin *columba*. St Columb Major was one of the wealthiest churches in Cornwall; St Coulm was venerated in Brittany and the name Kolumban is still in use there; and the sixth-century Columba was responsible for converting Scotland and Northern England to Christianity.

Colman is a form of the name Columbanus. As well as several hundred Irish saints called Colman, the name has been given to poets and priests, musicians and missionaries.

St Columba was also called *colm + cille*, Colmcille, or 'dove of the church'. He was born in Northern Ireland about 521 and became a monk under St Finnian. There are many legends about Columba but the most memorable relates to his copying a Bible. The monastery that owned the original Bible claimed the copy as its own, and the judgement of the highest court in the land decided: To every cow belongs its calf and to every book its copy, Columba went to war to keep his copy, but the battle at Cooldrebhne (*Cúl Dreimhne*) was so bloody that Columba decided to go into exile to atone for his sins and promised that he would never again as long as he lived 'set foot on Irish soil'. He founded a monastery at Iona which became the centre for Christianity in Scotland. According to legend, Columba longed to see Ireland again before he died but did not want to break his vow. So he filled his shoes with Scottish soil so that, although he was in his beloved Ireland, he never actually put his foot on Irish soil!

SEE: **Callum**

Colquhoun

SEE: **Calhoun**

Comhghal(l) (pronounced like 'co + all')

Comhghal(l) was a follower of Columba and went with him to Iona. His name may come from *comhghaol*, meaning 'close relative'. Like

Columba, he was renowned for his religious zeal in training missionaries for Europe.

Conaire (pronounced like 'con + oo + er'), **Conor, Conchobar, Conchubhar, Conchúr, Conchobarre** (pronounced like 'con + or', or 'con + oo + er')

These names are all variants of Con(n)or and may come from *conairt*, 'pack of hounds', and imply 'lover of hounds' or *conáire*, meaning 'hound-nobleman'. There are many Irish Conors, some saints, many sinners and at least two kings, namely Conaire who was king of Tara and Conchubhar MacNessa who was the king of Ulster and who, according to legend, was born on the same day as Christ. This Conchubhar was an uncle of Cúchulainn and was in love with Deirdre.

Conall, Connall, Connell

This Gaelic name comes from *con*, a prefix relating to 'hound' and meaning 'strong as an (Irish) hound', and it is popular as both a given name and a surname. One of the best-known holders of this name was Conall Cearnach (Conall the Victorious) who was a warrior almost as famous as his foster brother Cúchulainn.

Conan, Konan

This Gaelic name is probably a diminutive form of *con(n)* and, in the form *cónán*, means 'little wolf hound'. It was the middle name of Sir Arthur

Conan Doyle, the creator of Sherlock Holmes. An earlier Conan, sometimes called Conan Maol (Bald Conan), was a warrior companion of Fionn MacCool. Konan is the preferred form in Brittany.

Conchobar, Concubhar, Conchur, Conchobarre

SEE: **Conaire**

Conganchas (pronounced like 'con + gan + a + hiss')

Conganchas was thought to be an invincible warrior. His name may come from *cóngas*, 'drug, medication'. Thanks to a magic spell, no weapon could pierce his body. Niamh was persuaded to marry him so that she could find out the secret of his vulnerability. (There are parallels between her story and Delilah's: she discovered that he could only be mortally wounded if the sole of his foot was pierced by a spear.) The Breton names Kongar and Konogan may be related.

Conlan, Conlin, Conlon

These are variants that occur widely as a surname. The name may come from *connlán*, meaning 'endeavour', or it may be related to both Conlaoch and Conn.

Conlaoch, Conla, Conleth, Connla

Conlaoch comes from *conn + laoch*, meaning 'noble warrior, highest lord', and so was a term occasionally applied to Christ. One of the earliest holders of the name was the son of Cúchulainn and the Scottish queen Aoife. According to legend Cúchulainn killed his son without knowing who he was.

Conn

This was originally a name in its own right, in that the Irish word *conn* could mean 'noble one', but it is often thought to be a reduced form of Connor or Conall or Constantine. A famous Irish Conn was Conn Céad Cathach (Conn of the Hundred Battles).

Conall, Connell

SEE: **Conall**

Connla

SEE: **Conlaoch**

Conor, Connor

SEE: **Conaire**

Conway, Conwy

This name occurs in Ireland, Scotland, the Isle of Man and in Wales, where it is a place name. The Gaelic Conway is probably from *conn + mhaigh*, 'hound of the plain'. It shares part of its meaning with Connemara or 'hound of the sea'.

Corc, Corcoran, Corquoran

(pronounced like 'cork' and 'cor + cor + an')

The Gaelic adjective *corc*, meaning 'reddened' or 'singed', was the nickname of Conall MacLighthigh, who was fostered by a woman called Fidelma who had extraordinary

magical gifts. Corc went to Scotland where he married the daughter of the Pictish king but later returned to Ireland and became king of Munster. The monosyllabic name is no longer used but the longer, related names have been given as first names, especially to redheads.

Corentine, Chorentine (pronounced like 'cor + en + teen')

Corentine was an early Breton hermit who lived by a river and was, according to legend, fed by a miraculous fish that gave him a slice to eat every day. The meaning of his name is uncertain but the *cor-* may mean 'raven'. Corentine was honoured in Cornwall as Cury.

Corey, Cory

Corey, like many Irish surnames, was originally a first name, probably derived from the Germanic name *god + frid(d)*, Godfrey, meaning 'God's peace'. Its use may have been encouraged in Ireland by the Gaelic *cuairteoir*, 'visitor'.

Cormac, Cormack, Cormick

Cormac comes from *cor + mac* and means 'son of the raven'. The name is especially popular in Ireland and Scotland. There are several early references to Cormac. One was the high king of Ireland, Cormac Mac Airt, who was brought up by a she-wolf and was said to be the wisest man in the world. Another was the warrior son of Conchubhar MacNessa.

Cory

SEE: **Corey**

Coulm

SEE: **Colm**

Craiftín, Críomhtán (pronounced like 'craft + een' and 'cree + if + tawn')

These may be distinct Gaelic names although they are both often related to 'fox'. Craiftín may also come from *cráibhtheach + ín*, meaning 'little devout one'. An Irish Craiftín was a harper of such excellence that his music could lull anyone into a trance-like state. It is possible that Críomhtán was Columba's original name.

Craig

Craig, like Carraig, comes from the Gaelic word *carraig*, meaning 'rock'. It is popular in Scotland, America and Australia and is the given name of the former *Neighbours* star, Craig McLaughlin.

Credne, Creidne (pronounced to rhyme with 'sedge + nih')

It is far from certain what Credne's name means, although it may be related to *creidsin*, 'belief'. According to legend, Credne was a smith who made weapons for the gods and who was so skilled as a silversmith that he helped to make a silver hand for Nuada when he lost his hand in battle.

Críomhtán

SEE: **Craiftín**

Crionnchú

SEE: **Crunnchú**

Cronán, Cronin

Cronán seems to come from *crón* and to mean 'sallow, dark-complexioned'. The seventh-century saint Cronán was a dedicated worker for the poor and the homeless.

Crunnchú, Crionnchú (pronounced like 'croon + oo + hoo')

Crunnchú seems to be related to the Gaelic word *críonna*, meaning 'prudent', although this adjective may have been used satirically. Crunnchú was a mortal from Armagh who was loved by Macha, a goddess. She lived with him as his wife but warned him that he must not tell anyone of her supernatural powers. But Crunnchú boasted that his pregnant wife could run faster than the king's fastest horse. The race was organised and Macha won, giving birth to twins on the finishing line. Macha had to leave her husband, but she gave her name to Armagh or Árd Mhacha.

Cubi, Cybi (pronounced like 'cube + ee')

Cubi was the son of a third- or fourth-century Cornish warrior. He became a Christian and travelled to France where he became bishop of Poitiers. His name may be related to *cú*, 'hound'.

Cúchulainn, Cúchulain, CúChulain (pronounced like 'coo + hull + in')

Cúchulainn is probably the best known of all Irish warrior heroes. His name was originally Setanta but his nickname *cú* + *chulainn* means 'hound of Culann'. He earned it when, as a boy, he killed Culann's hound and promised to act as Culann's guard until he had managed to train a new hound. Cúchulainn trained as a warrior in both Ireland and Scotland, fought with the Red Branch Knights, and single-handedly defended Ulster against the might of Queen Maeve's army.

Cuirithír (pronounced like 'coo + er + eer')

We cannot be certain what this name means although it may be related to *cúirt*, 'palace', or *cuirthe*, 'put off'. The story of Cuirithír and Liadin is one of the great love stories of Irish tradition. They were both poets and, although they loved each other, Liadin decided to become a nun. When Cuirithír failed to make her change her mind, he left Ireland and became a monk. They never saw each other again although, in some versions of their story, they were reunited in heaven.

Culhwch (pronounced like 'cool + (h)ooh')

Culhwch's name may be related to *cylch*, 'circle', but it is said to be derived from an Old Welsh compound meaning 'controller of pigs'. Culhwch was the nephew of King Arthur. His mother was determined that her son should control the animal that had frightened her when she was pregnant.

Cullan, Cullen, Cullin

It is likely that this name is a diminutive of *coll*, 'chieftain'.

Curran

This popular surname probably comes from *cath*, 'battle', and means 'brave warrior, hero'. It has begun to be used as a first name.

Cybi

SEE: **Cubi**

Cynog (pronounced like 'kin + og')

SEE: **Canank**

Dacey

The name comes from Gaelic *deas* and means 'southern'.

SEE: **Desmond**

Dafydd

SEE: **Dai**

Dagda, Daghda (pronounced like 'die + da')

Dagda or Daghda was an Irish god and his name *dagh* + *dia* means 'good, kind god'. He was noted in particular for his ability to play three types of harp music: one that would make all who heard it sad, one that would make everyone happy, and one that would make everyone sleep. He used the last type of music to overcome his enemies without shedding blood.

Dagonet

Dagonet was King Arthur's court jester, but he showed in battle that he had courage as well as wit. His name seems to be related to *dagreuol*, meaning 'tearful', although it may have been modified in line with Dagobert, the name of a French king.

Dai, Dáibhí, Dafydd, Davet, David, Davie, Davy, Devi, Dewi, Divi, Tafydd

David was the name of the king of the Israelites, as told in the Book of Samuel. It means 'beloved, darling' and has been popular worldwide. The patron saint of Wales is David and Scotland had two kings with the name. Dáibhí, Davet, David, Davie and Davy are used in Ireland; Devi, Divi and Dewi occur in Brittany; Dafydd, David, Davie, Davy, Dewi and Tafydd are used in Wales; and Scotland and the Isle of Man tend to use David, Davie and Davy. The Welsh pronunciation of Dafydd was often heard as Tafydd and, since the name was so popular in Wales, 'Taffy' came to be used to represent any Welshman in the same way that 'Paddy' was used for an Irishman or 'Jock' for a Scot.

Dáire, Darry, Dary (pronounced like 'daw + ir + ih')

Dáire was a Gaelic god, whose name *dáire* means 'fruitful'.

Dáithí, Dahey, Dahy, Dathy
(pronounced like 'dah + hee' or 'daw + hee')

Dáithí is sometimes interpreted as a form of Dáibhí but Gaelic *daithe* mean 'swiftness, nimbleness'. It was the name of a fifth-century Irish king whose warlike adventures are similar to those of King Arthur. The name occurs most frequently as a surname.

Dálaigh, Dálach, Daley, Daly
(pronounced like 'dawl + ee' or 'dale + ee')

This name is said to be related to the Irish word *dáil*, 'meeting, parliament', and to refer, therefore, to a 'counsellor' or, less romantically, to someone who goes to meetings. It is used widely as a surname and has been popularised as a first name by the Olympic decathlete, Daley Thompson.

Dalzell, Dalziel(l) (pronounced like 'dee + yell')

This Celtic name is no longer widely used but it is attractive in form and meaning, suggesting 'farmer, cultivator of the land'.

Daniel, Dan, Danny, Deniel

Daniel is not a Celtic name but comes from Hebrew where it meant 'God is my judge'. The biblical Daniel was expert at interpreting dreams, a skill that was highly prized by the Celts, and so his name was adopted and adapted by them. The pet form Dan was particularly attractive to Gaelic speakers because of its association with *dán*, 'poetry', and Danny almost became Irish because of the song 'Danny Boy'. Deniel is found in

Brittany and the feminine form Danni has begun to be used.

Dara (pronounced like 'dar + ra'), **Darach, Daragh, Darrach, Darragh**

These variants all come from a Gaelic word *dara*, meaning 'like oak'. The '-*ach*' forms are popular in Scotland and the others are preferred in Ireland. The name Dara is being used as a girl's name because of the tendency of '-*a*' to signal a female in some European languages.
SEE: **Dara, Deri**

Darby, Derby

Darby was popular in Ireland, where it was often regarded as a form of Diarmuid or Dermot, possibly from *di + airmait*, meant 'without + envy'.
SEE: **Diarmad**

D'Arcy, Dorsey

A number of French names were adopted into Irish shortly after the Norman Conquest. Since they have been used in the country for close on 900 years, they can be classified as Irish, especially since they were often equated with a similar sounding Irish name. D'Arcy, which meant 'from Arcy', is probably a form of *dorchaidhe*, meaning 'dark haired'. This is also sometimes anglicised as Dorsey.

Darrach, Darragh
SEE: **Dara**

Daren, Darin, Darran, Darren

This name is currently popular and so appears in a variety of spellings. It seems likely that it is a diminutive of *dara* and thus means 'little oak'.

Darry, Dary
SEE: **Dáire**

Dathy
SEE: **Dáithí**

Davet, David, Davie, Davy
SEE: **Dai**

Dawe, Docco, Dochau, Docwina

The Welsh saint Dawe (or occasionally Docco, Dochau and Docwina) lived in the fifth century and gave his name to the church of Llandochau Fawr in Glamorgan. It seems probable that the saint established a monastery on the north coast of Cornwall, where the church of St Kew was originally dedicated to St Docco. The meaning of the name is debated but it may be related to *tawelwch* and mean 'calm' or it may be an early form of David, meaning 'beloved'.

Deaglán, Declán (pronounced like 'deg + lawn' and 'deck + lawn'), **Declan** (pronounced like 'deck + lan')

Deaglán or Declan seems to have been one of the first Irish Christians and may have preached in Ireland before the arrival of St Patrick. It is not certain what the name means although it may be related to *deagh*, 'good' + *lán*, 'full', suggesting 'full of goodness'.

Deasmhumhain, Deasún
SEE: **Desmond**

Deimhne
SEE: **Demne**

Delaney, Delany
Delaney is most widely used as an Irish surname related to *deagh-laoch*, meaning 'challenger, trained warrior'. It is beginning to be used as a given name.

Demne, Deimhne (pronounced like 'dem + nee' and 'dev + neh')
Demne was the childhood name of Fionn MacCool. Its meaning is uncertain but it may relate to *deimhne*, 'assurance, proof'. It is interesting to note how often changes are made to the names of people who are destined to be great or memorable. Abram became Abraham, Simon became Peter, Setanta became Cúchulainn and Demne became Fionn.
SEE: **Finn**

Dempsey
Dempsey may be related to a placename *domasach*, 'place of light soil', although many people of this name suggest otherwise. In some cultures, pride was not necessarily seen as a weakness. Dempsey may mean 'the proud one' but the pride would be regarded as justified.

Deniel
SEE: **Daniel**

Denzel, Denzell, Denzil, Donasien
Denzel(l) is a Cornish surname possibly related to *danas*, 'fallow deer', although the first syllable may have a link with the goddess Don. It is also possible that it is a Celtic form of Dionysus, the god of wine. The name has been adopted in a number of spellings and was introduced to a wider audience by the American actor, Denzel Washington.
SEE: **Dionnsaidhe**

Derby
SEE: **Darby**

Dermot, Dermott
SEE: **Diarmad**

Derry
Derry is used as an abbreviation of Andrew, Derek, Dermot and, less often, Desmond, but it has a meaning in its own right and, as *daraigh*, can suggest 'like an oak'.

Desmond, Deasmhumhain, Deasún
Desmond was originally a regional classification meaning 'one from south Munster or *Deas Mumhan*'. The anglicised ending is due to influence from such names as Esmond and Richmond. Desmond has several popular diminutives, including Des, Dessie, Desy, Dez and Dezzy.

See: Dacey

Devi, Dewi
SEE: **Dai**

Devin, Devon

This name, which is popular in the Caribbean, may come from the name of the English county or from a Celtic words, *dán*, 'gift', or *dána*, meaning 'intrepid'.

Devlin

This Irish surname was originally a nickname meaning 'strong and courageous'. It is, thus, an attractive option for a given name.

Dewey, Dewi

SEE: **Dai**

Diancecht (pronounced like 'dee + in + kecht')

Diancecht comes from *dianchéacht*, 'god of medicine'. He was the grandfather of the king and warrior Lugh. He was the skilled doctor who, according to legend, helped to make a silver hand to replace the one lost by Nuada in battle. He also had the power to bless water so that anyone who drank from it would be immediately refreshed in body and mind.

Diarmad, Diarmaid, Diarmait, Diarmid, Diarmuid, Dermot, Dermott

This name occurs in a wide number of forms. The Diar- forms are found in Scotland, Ireland and, to a lesser extent, the Isle of Man, and the Der- forms are popular worldwide as both first names and, with Mac, as surnames. The name probably comes from *di + airmait*, meaning 'without envy', and it has been held by warriors, kings and saints. Perhaps the best-known bearer of the name was the young warrior hero who fell in love with Gráinne. (Legend has it that this Dermot had a 'love spot' that made him irresistible to women. Unfortunately, no details survive!) As in many Gaelic stories, Gráinne was already promised, in her case to the aged Fionn MacCool. They ran away together and had sixteen years of happiness before returning to Ireland to face Fionn's wrath.

Dillon

Dillon may be related to *dealán*, 'streak of light', or it may mean 'faithful, loyal'. It is widely used as a surname in Ireland and is occasionally equated with Welsh Dylan.

SEE: **Dylan**

Dionnsaidhe, Dionnsaí (pronounced like 'done + she')

Dionnsaidhe is an Irish form of Den(n)is and comes ultimately from the Greek name Dionysius, which meant 'devoted follower of god'. The name has been popular since the third century when a St Denis converted France and became the patron saint of Paris. The Bretons use a similar name, Dinan. Dinny is occasionally used as a diminutive.

Diuran (pronounced like 'dee + your + an'), Diurán

Diuran or Diurán was one of the young men who accompanied Maeldún on his *Immrama*. Diuran's name may be associated with *diúrnán*, 'gulp, sip of liquid', and an explanation for this may be found in oral versions of his story. Diuran had been badly scarred during the voyage and was physically at a low ebb when he and his companions saw an old phoenix dive into a crater lake and come out rejuvenated. While the others wondered what to do, Diuran leapt into the lake and, as he drank and swam, his body was totally renewed. The magical powers of the lake only lasted for a few minutes, however, and so by the time the others decided it was safe to follow Diuran's example, the water had lost its potency.

Divi
See: **Dai**

Diwrnach, Dyrnwch (pronounced like 'dew + er + nootch')
This Welsh giant's name may be associated with *diwarafun*, meaning 'unstinting', although this is not certain. He seems to have been the steward of the King of Ireland and to have possessed a pot that refused to cook the food of a coward.

Docco, Dochan, Dowrina
SEE: **Dawe**

Dod, Dodie
These abbreviations are sometimes used in Scotland and are usually given to a boy whose name is David.
SEE: **Dan**

Dogmael, Dogmeel

Very little is known about St Dogmael except that churches were dedicated to him in Brittany and Cornwall. The name is no longer popular but the saint's day is still celebrated in Brittany on 14 June.
SEE: **Dogmaela**

Dolan, Doyle
The meaning of the Irish surname Dolan is not absolutely clear although it may be from *dubh*, 'black', and have been a nickname for someone with black hair. In this respect, it would overlap with Doyle and be a variant of Dubhlainn.

Domhnal(l), Donal, Donald
At one time Donald was second only to Ian as the most popular male name in Scotland, but it suffered a decline thanks in part to the success of the Disney character, Donald Duck. The earlier form of the Gaelic name, Domhnal(l), helps us to see its meaning of 'ruler of the world' in that *domhan* is 'world'. It has been the given name of poets and saints.

Donn
Donn was an Irish adjective meaning 'brown' and also 'princely', but it is likely that the name Donn is linked to the mother god, Donn. According to Gaelic folklore, Donn was, like the Greek god Pluto, the guardian of the 'underworld'. Such a term hides the fact, however, that the ancient Irish dead did not go underground. Rather, they went to an island, that was a stepping stone on the way to the

islands of the blessed, where the good went. The link between islands and the hereafter was a pagan tradition that the Irish Christians took over. It partly explains the attraction of places like Lough Derg, or St Patrick's Purgatory, a little island where the living go to make reparation for any sins in their life. The pet names Don and Donnie are likely to come from Donald.

Donncha (pronounced like 'done + ah + ha'), Donnchadh, Don(n)ach, Don(n)agh, Don(n)ough

These names are variants of a Gaelic noun *donnchadh*, meaning 'brown-haired warrior', and are all beginning to find renewed popularity after a period when they were mainly found in versions of the surname Donaghy. One traditional story is told about how a Donncha fought with death and held him at bay until death could be tricked into releasing him.

SEE: **Duncan**

Donovan

Like many ancient Irish first names, Donovan was preserved by becoming a surname. It is a combination of *donn*, meaning 'brown' or 'princely', and *dubh*, meaning 'black', plus a diminutive marker, suggesting that it may have been a nickname originally, meaning either 'little dark one' or 'little dark prince'. The name was given a new lease of life by the American folk singer, Donovan.

Doogan

SEE: **Dugan**

Doran, Dorian

Doran comes from *deoadhán* and seems to mean 'the exiled one'. It is relatively common as a surname but is becoming attractive too as a given name. It is possible that this name influenced Wilde's choice of Dorian in *The Portrait of Dorian Gray*.

SEE: **Dorian, Dorien**

Dorsey

SEE: **D'Arcy**

Dougal, Dubhgal(l), Dugald

The Irish distinguished between the Viking invaders from Norway, whom they called *Fionn + gall*, meaning 'fair stranger', and the Danes, whom they called *dubh + gall*, meaning 'dark stranger'. Dougal became a popular first name, especially in Scotland. It seems likely that the surname Doyle is a form of Dubhgall and it, too, has been used as a given name.

Dougan

See: **Dugan**

Douglas

The name Douglas comes from the Gaelic elements *dubh + glas*, meaning 'black + water', a name that was given to several rivers and to the capital of the Isle of Man. It is used also as a surname in Scotland, where the Douglas clan has been powerful since the twelfth century. Their motto is *jamais arrière*, 'never in the rear'.

Drew

Drew is normally an abbreviation of Andrew, coming originally from Greek *andreas*, meaning 'warrior'. It is possible, however, that it is a Celtic name in its own right, related to *draoi*, 'dealer in magic' and Druid, 'wise one'.

Drustan (pronounced like 'drew + stan')

This is a variant of Tristan and may be the older form. It is possible that the name is a variant of Druce, a form of *draoi*, 'magic, wise' and thus means 'son of the wise'. Tristan, the tragic lover of Iseult (Yseult), may have gained the Tr- form of his name because *triste* means 'sad'.

SEE: **Tristan, Yseult**

Duane, Dwayne

Duane means 'dark little one' and comes from the Gaelic name *Dubhán*, which is also anglicised as Duffin. The name was popularised by the singer Duane Eddy and occurs also in the forms Dwane and Dwayne. It is perhaps most popular today in the Caribbean.

Dougan

SEE: **Duana**

Dubhgal(l)

SEE: **Dougal**

Dubhlainn, Doolin

This name, which involves Gaelic *dubh*, 'black' and possibly mean 'black blade', was held by the lover of Aoibhell, whose harp playing was legendary. According to prophecy, Dubhlainn should have died in battle, but Aoibhell loved him so much that she wove him a cloak that made him invisible.

Dugald

This form of Dougal is found almost exclusively in Scotland and Northern Ireland.

SEE: **Dougal**

Dugan, Doogan, Dougan

Dugan is occasionally spelt Doogan or Dougan. All of the variants relate to dubh, 'black', and suggest 'dark-haired'.

Duncan

Duncan is a form of *donn* + *cha(dh)*, meaning 'princely battle' or, more likely, 'brown-haired warrior'. It is now most popular in Scotland, where it was the name of the king murdered by Macbeth. It was also held by both an Irish and a Scottish saint.

SEE: **Dominica, Donncha**

Dunstan

Dunstan is usually thought of as a Germanic name meaning 'dark stone', but the Gaelic adjective *donn* meaning 'brown' or 'princely' and the name Drustan may have contributed to its popularity.

Dylan, Dillon

Dylan has become very popular in the twentieth century. It probably comes from a poetic Welsh noun meaning 'sea'. He was the son of Arianrhod, who taught poets. More recently, the name has been held by the Welsh poet, Dylan Thomas, whose work is renowned for its rhythms and its creative use of language.

Dyrnwch
SEE: **Diwrnach**

Eacha, Eachann (pronounced like 'ah + ha' or 'ak + ha')
These names come from Gaelic *each*, meaning 'horse', and probably imply that the bearer was either an excellent horseman or possibly even a god. In Scotland, Eacha Donn or Eachdhonn was equated with Hector, the Trojan champion, renowned for his skill as a horseman.

Eamon, Éamon, Eamonn, Éamonn (pronounced like 'aim + an')
Eamon(n) is the Irish equivalent of Old English *ead + mund*, Edmond or Edmund, and the name means 'prosperity and protection'.

Éareamhóin, Éireamhóin
(pronounced like 'air + a + vone'), **Eremon, Ervin Erwan, Erwin, Irwin**
Éireamhóin was a Milesian and the brother of Éibhear. His name is often anglicised as Ervin, Erwan, Erwin or Irwin and so equated with an English name that means 'boar friend'. In Scotland, the names Irvine and Irving are not seen as related to Éareamhóin but are thought to come from the placename near Dumfries. Erwin

occurs also in Wales partly because of the sound similarity between Old English *wine*, 'friend', and Welsh *(g)wyn*, 'white, fair'. Bretons use the form Erwan but this overlaps with their use of Evan for John.
SEE: **Éibhear, Eremon**

Easal (pronounced like 'ah + sal')
Easal, whose name may be linked in meaning to *eas*, 'waterfall', was a king who owned seven pigs whose great attraction was that, if they were killed and eaten at night, they were found alive and well in their sty the next morning.

Eber (pronounced like 'ey + ber' or 'ee + ber')
SEE: **Éibhear**

Edan
Edan is an unusual but attractive version of Aidan, from *aodh + ín*, meaning 'little fire, flame'.

Edern (pronounced like 'aid + ern' or 'ee + dern')
Edern is a Breton name, thought to be a modified form of Germanic *ead + weard*, Edward, meaning 'guardian of prosperity'. Although Edward is originally English, it became popular throughout Europe after the death of St Edward the Confessor (1066) and we can still find Eduardos in Spain and Duartes in Portugal.

Edryd
Edryd is a Welsh name meaning 'restoring'. It may also relate to Welsh *eddryd*, 'story-teller'.

Efflam

Efflam defeated a large serpent that King Arthur could not subdue. His name may be related to Welsh *effro*, 'vigilant'. The name is used in Brittany where St Efflam's feast day is celebrated on 6 November.

Efnissien (pronounced like 'eff + niss + ee + an')

People in many communities often give twins similar names. Efnissien's name meant 'not at peace' and his brother was Nissien or 'peaceful'. Efnissien was the son of Penarddun and Euroswydd and he objected to the marriage of his sister, Branwen, to the Irish king because he feared that the sovereignty of the British kingdom might pass to the Irish through the female line.

SEE: **Éibhear, Nissien**

Egan, Egin, Eginer, Iagan (pronounced like 'ey + gan' or 'ee + gan')

Originally, Egan was written Aodhgan and was probably a pet form of Aodh or Aidan and thus meant 'little fire'. The name has given rise to the surnames Hagan and O'Hagan, and Hagan is occasionally used as a first name too. There is a Scottish form Iagan and a Breton equivalent Eginer, which also has Fingar as a pet form.

Eglamour (pronounced like 'eg + la + moor')

Eglamour's name almost certainly involves the French noun *amour*,

meaning 'love' and the stories associated with him show why it is appropriate. Eglamour was poor but he loved Crystabel, who was the daughter of a powerful knight. Eglamour had to slay a giant, a boar and a dragon in order to prove his love, and, just when it looked as if he and his lover would be united, their son was stolen by a griffin!

Éibhear, Eber (pronounced like 'aye + ver')

Éibhear had a brother and they were reputed to be Milesians, or early settlers in Ireland, a fact that is clear if we look closely at the names. Éibhear is an Irish version of Latin *Hibernia*, 'winter country', and Éireamhóin's name includes Éire the Irish name for Ireland. Scholars now dispute the accuracy of many of the legends of settlement but the names are attractive. Yves is occasionally used as a variant of Éibhear.

SEE: **Effnissien, Éareamhóin**

Eiros

Eiros is Welsh and means 'bright'. It may come from *eira*, meaning 'snow'.

Elath, Elatha (pronounced like 'ay + lath + a')

Elatha was a handsome young prince who fell in love with a beautiful Irish goddess, Éire. Because of their different backgrounds, they could not get married but Elatha gave the goddess a ring for their son, Bres. Later, when Bres needed support, he showed the ring to his father and was successful in his quest. It is not apparent what Elatha means but it seems to be related to *ealadha*, meaning 'skill, learning'.

Elcmar (pronounced like 'elk + mar')

Elcmar was the husband of the goddess Boann. His name seems to be related to *ealga*, meaning 'noble'. Elcmar was deposed by Aengus in much the same way as Kronos (Saturn) was ousted by Zeus (Jupiter) in Greek mythology.

Elfed

This Welsh name, which means 'autumn harvest', is experiencing renewed popularity.

Eliaz

SEE: Ellis

Elidr, El(l)idor

Gerald of Wales (otherwise known as Giraldus Cambrensis) wrote *The History and Topography of Ireland* in Latin and tells a story in it of a beautiful boy called Elidr, possibly related to *alaeth*, 'sorrow'. Every day he used to play with the gods and goddesses and one of their games involved a golden ball. His mother asked him where he went and when he confided in her, she told him to bring back the golden ball. Elidor did this and was never again able to pass between the two worlds.

SEE: Aled

Eliot, Elliot

Eliot possibly comes from the Hebrew name Elias, meaning 'the Lord is God'. It is the name of a Borders family in Scotland, whose famous ancestor, Gilbert or 'Gibbie wi' the gowden garters', was convicted of High Treason for plotting against the Catholic king, James II. Fortunately for his descendants, he was pardoned and later became Lord Minto.

Ellis, Elisud, Eliaz

Ellis is a Welsh name, thought to be a reduced form of *elisud*, which means 'benevolent'. The Welsh name has been influenced in spelling by the English surname Ellis, which comes from the Biblical Elias or Elijah, meaning 'Jehovah is God'. There is a Breton form Eliaz.

Elouan

SEE: Elwin

Elphin

This Welsh name may be related to *elus*, 'kind', influenced by English *elf*, which seems to be related to Latin *albus*, 'white'. Elphin was the son of Gwyddno and was thought to be the unluckiest young man in the world. Once, when he was fishing, he caught a coracle containing the poet, Taliesin, and from that moment his luck changed. He had a horse that could outrun any other, a wife who was the most beautiful in the world, and he found a pot of gold which could never be emptied.

Elvi

Elvi was a saint who lived in Wales and is reputed to have baptised St Dewi (David) in the fifth century. It seems possible that Elvi was Irish and that his name was possibly Alban from Latin *albus*, 'white, pure'.

Elwin, Elouan

Elwin occurs as a first name and may be a blend of *elus* + *gwyn*, meaning 'kind + fair'. Its Breton equivalent is Elouan but the names are much closer in pronunciation than the spelling suggests if we remember that French *oui* is pronounced like English *we*.

Emlyn, Emilion

Emlyn is probably a Welsh form of Latin *aemulus*, meaning 'rival', although it may also have been influenced by the biblical name Emmanuel, meaning 'God is with us'. The Breton name Emilion, or occasionally Million, has been influenced by French Émile, which is from the same Latin source and means 'industrious'.

Emmet

Emmet is a good example of a name that is Irish by adoption, thanks to the patriot Robert Emmet, who was a leader of the 1798 rebellion and whose speech from the dock 'Let no-one write my epitaph' is perhaps the most moving in the English language. The name Emmet is an English surname. It comes from an Old English word *oemette*, 'ant', and some English dialects still use 'emmet' with this meaning. The name is given to boys as a mark of respect for Robert Emmet.

Emrys (pronounced like 'em + riss')

Emrys is a Welsh form of Ambrose, from Greek *ambrosios*, meaning 'immortal'. It is popular in Wales and in Welsh communities, including Patagonia, South America, where a group of Welsh immigrants keeps the Welsh language and culture alive.

Enda

Enda or Éanna comes from Gaelic *éan*, meaning 'bird'. The best-known Enda was a warrior and a monk in the sixth century. He trained in Ireland and in Galloway, Scotland, before returning to Ireland.
SEE: **Fainche**

Ennis

Ennis is a placename in Ireland that has probably given rise to this boy's name. It may mean 'sole choice' or it may come from *innis*, 'island'. It is possible also that the name was reinforced by Aeneas, the hero of Troy, who is reputed to have founded Rome and whose name means 'greatly praised'.

Eochaidh (pronounced like 'och + he' or 'yoch + he')

Eochaidh comes from the Gaelic word *each*, meaning 'horse' and probably implying 'horse rider or trainer'. There are saints, a king and at least one poet called Eochaidh and the name seems to have developed into the surname Haughey, which is occasionally used as a first name. Although dictionaries do not acknowledge it, Eochaidh may well be the source of the English word 'jockey'.

Eoghan, Eoin, Erwan, Euan, Ewen, Owen (pronounced like 'oh + wen')

Variants of this name occur in all parts of the Celtic world. We have Eoghan in Ireland and Scotland, Ewen and Owen in Wales, Ewen and Youenn in Brittany, Eoin in Ireland and the Isle of Man, and the variants overlap with forms of John. It is uncertain where the name originated. It seems likely that it may have come from an old Celtic word for 'yew tree' and it may have been influenced by the name Eugene, which comes from Greek *eugenios*, meaning 'noble' and was held by a seventh-century pope. In Northern Ireland, the name Eoghan (which is found in Tyrone or *Tír Eoghain*) is often accompanied by Roe in memory of the Irish patriot Eoghan Ruadh O'Neill.

Eremon
SEE: Éareamhóin

Ernan, Ernie, Iarnan
This name comes from the Gaelic word *iarann*, 'iron', a metal that was held in high esteem for its durability. The name is now often linked with

Ernest, a Germanic name meaning 'seriousness'.

Ervin
SEE: Éareamhóin

Erwan, Erwin
SEE: Éareamhóin

Esras (pronounced like 'ess + rass') Esras was a magician, in the same mould as Merlin. He did not perform tricks but he was in possession of knowledge that gave him powers beyond other people. Many of the Celts admired courage and strength, but they had a great respect for knowledge. Esras had a spear that guaranteed victory to the leader who held it. The meaning of his name is debated but it may be related to 'proscribe, empower'.

Euan (pronounced like 'you + an')
SEE: Eoghan, Evan

Eudav
Eudav was, according to legend, the son of Caradoc and the father of Helena, who is sometimes equated with the mother of the Roman Emperor, Constantine.

Eurwyn
This Welsh name is the male equivalent of Eurwen and seems to be a blend of *euraid* + *gwyn*, meaning 'golden fair' or 'fair as gold'.

Evan, Evin, Ewan
Evan is considered to be Welsh and is, like Ieuan, a form of John and means 'God is gracious'. Evan and

Even are used also in Brittany where they are linked with John the Baptist. These forms overlap in Ireland and Scotland with forms of Eoghan, which are sometimes Ewan, Euan or Ewen. The Irish Evin does not seem to be related historically, since it means 'swift', but it is usual now to equate the names.

SEE: **Eoghan**

Fachnan (pronounced like 'foh + nan' or 'fok + nan')

Fachnan is a Gaelic name that can be either male or female. It probably comes from fach, 'challenge' and may imply 'hostile'. Fachnan was the name of a sixth-century Irish saint.

Fagan

This is well-known as an Irish surname because of the song 'Hello Patsy Fagan' and because of the character in *Oliver Twist* by Charles Dickens. The meaning of Fagan is not absolutely clear. It may come from *fiach* + *Egan*, meaning 'Egan's raven' or it may be a modified form of *fiach*, 'raven'.

Fanch, Fransez, Soaz

These are all Breton forms of Francis, meaning 'Frenchman' or 'from France'.

Faolán, Felan, Phelan (pronounced like 'fway' + lawn' or 'feel + an')

Faolán may come from *faoileann*, 'seagull', although it is often claimed

to mean 'wolf'. The Fenian character called Faolán was the epitome of loyalty.

Farquhar, Farquar, Fearchar

Farquar probably comes from *fear* + *cara*, meaning 'friendly man'. It is most frequently found in Scotland, where the surname Farquarson is also widespread. The Farquarson clan value their Celtic origins and are particularly proud of a female member of the clan, called Anne. She was called *La Belle Rebelle* because she roused the clan and ambushed a troop that was sent to capture Bonnie Prince Charlie.

Farrell, Ferrel(l)

Farrell occurs widely in Ireland as a surname. It comes from *fearghal* and means 'brave one'. It is an anglicisation of Fergal.

Fearchar

SEE: **Farquhar**

Fearghal, Fergal (pronounced like 'far + rell' and 'fer + gull')

There is some debate about the meaning of Fergal but it seems to be from *fearghal* and to mean 'brave, courageous, valorous'. This name is occasionally used as an Irish equivalent of Virgil, a Latin name that meant 'strong and prosperous'.

Fearghas, Fearghus, Feargus, Fergus (pronounced like 'far + a + gas' or 'fer + guss')

These names are growing in popularity. Their meaning is debated but is probably derived from *fearr*, 'best', or *fear*, 'man', or *fearr + gas*, 'best warrior'. The first variant is used mainly in Ireland, the second in Scotland but Fergus is the preferred form worldwide. According to legend, Fergus was the king of Ulster and Nessa implored him to let her son Conchubhar rule in his place for a year. Fergus agreed but Conchubhar refused to relinquish the throne and so Fergus joined Maeve in her battle against Ulster.

Felim, Felimy
SEE: **Phelim, Phelimy**

Felix, Filis
Felix is a Latin name, *felix* meaning 'the lucky one' and it is still popular in parts of Ireland, Scotland and Brittany, where Filis is used.

Fenit, Fianaid, Fianait
This Gaelic name means 'little deer'. It is also the name of a place in Kerry near Tralee and is perhaps more frequently given as a girl's name.

Ferdia, Ferdiad
The meaning of Ferdia or Ferdiad is not certain but it may come from *fear + Dia* and mean 'man of God'. What is certain is that he and Cúchulainn were close friends. Ferdia was from Connacht, whereas his friend was an Ulsterman. When Queen Maeve of Connaught went to war with Ulster, Cúchulainn guarded the ford and Ferdia was forced to meet him in single combat. They fought during

sunlight hours for three days. At sunset each day, they put down their weapons and treated each other's wounds. The following morning, they greeted each other as friends before fighting again. It became clear that neither would gain the upper hand and so Cúchulainn had to use a magical spear, which no-one could withstand. In this way, Cúchulainn eventually overcame Ferdia.

Fergal
SEE: **Feargal**

Fergus
SEE: **Fearghas**

Ferguson
Ferguson is occasionally used as a first name in Scotland and Northern Ireland, where the surname is quite widely found. The Fergus(s)ons trace their clan back to a twelfth-century Fergus, or *fearghas* 'great warrior' and their motto can be translated as 'Sweeter after difficulties'.

Ferrel, Ferrell
SEE: **Farrell**

Ferris
This Gaelic name probably comes from *a Phiarais*, a form borrowed from Norman 'Piers' meaning both 'Peter' and 'rock'. It is quite widely found as a surname but seems to be growing in popularity as a given name. A very similar sounding name, Ferrishin, is used in the Isle of Man for the *Sidhe* or fairy people.

Fiachna (pronounced like 'fee + ach + nah')

Fiachna's name also seems to be a version of fiach, 'raven'. He was the son of king Lír and brother of Fionnuala.

Fiachra, Fiacre, Fiakr (pronounced like 'fee + ach + rih')

These variants are found in Ireland and Brittany. Fiachra comes from *fiach*, meaning 'raven', a bird that was sacred to the Celts, and an early Irish hermit called Fiachra went to live in Northern France.

Fianaid, Fianai
SEE: **Fenit**

Fife, Fyfe

This name comes from Fife in Scotland and so meant 'person from Fife'. It became well known as a first name because of the Scottish broadcaster, Fyfe Robinson.

Filis
SEE: **Felix**

Finan, Fíonán

This Gaelic name seems to be from Latin *vinum*, 'wine', although it may have been influenced by *Fionn*, meaning 'white, fair'.

Finbar, Fionnbar(r), Fymber

This attractive boy's name probably comes from *fi(o)nn + bearr*, meaning 'fair-headed'. The name has been popular since the sixth century and St Finbar of Cork had cult status in Cornwall, under the name of Fymber.

Findlay, Findley, Finlay

Finlay means 'fair-haired hero' and deserves to be more widely used as a first name. The surname gained a wide degree of recognition because of the long-running television series, *Dr Findlay's Casebook*.

Fingal, Fion(n)gall

Fingal was the nickname used by the Irish and the Scots to describe the Norwegian Vikings. The name means 'fair stranger' and was in contrast to Dougal or 'dark stranger', the name that was given to the Danes. Fingal is occasionally used in Scotland for Fionn MacCool.

Fingus
SEE: **Finnegas**

Finian
SEE: **Finnian**

Finlay
SEE: **Findlay**

Finn, Fionn

Finn or Fionn means 'fair-haired' and the most famous Fionn to date is Fionn MacCool, the legendary leader of the Fianna, a warrior band composed of 150 chieftains and approximately 4,000 warriors, musicians, poets, priests and physicians. Fionn was not only incredibly strong, but he was also extremely wise. He had acquired his wisdom by touching the salmon of knowledge and then sucking his thumb.

Finnegas, Fingus

Finnegas, which seems to come from *finn* + *geas* and means 'fair-haired man of vigour', was a poet and the mentor of Fionn MacCool. Finnegas was in charge of the salmon of all knowledge. Whoever ate the salmon would not only know the past, but the future too. When he was roasting the salmon on a spit, Fionn MacCool touched it, sucked his thumb and was immediately filled with more knowledge than he knew what to do with.

Finnian, Finian

Finnian is thought to mean 'fair-headed' and it may be a blend of Gaelic *finn* and Welsh or Cornish *gwyn*. Saying the same thing in two languages is not unusual. We find it in 'flagstone' (flag = stone) and in 'pussycat'. The name is popular and became even more so after the making of the film *Finian's Rainbow*.

Fintan, Fiontan

Fintan is one of the many Gaelic names coming from *finn* or *fionn* and referring to fair hair. It is the equivalent of 'fair-haired one'. There have been many saints with this name, including one who lived most of his short life on a diet of bread and water.

Fíonán

SEE: **Finan**

Fion(n)gall

SEE: **Fingal**

Fionn

SEE: **Finn**

Fionnbar, Fionnbarr

SEE: **Finbar**

Fiontan

SEE: **Fintan**

Flann, Flannagan

Flann means 'bright red' and its use was popularised by the writer Flann O'Brien, whose novel *At Swim-Two-Birds* was published in 1939. Flannagan is a pet form of the name.

Floyd

Floyd is a variant of Lloyd, from *llwyd*, which means 'grey-haired'. (The Celts often classified people by the colour or texture of their hair.) The 'Fl-' is an English method of trying to reproduce the voiceless Welsh alveolar fricative *the*, that is represented by 'll'. For the same reason, Shakespeare used the name Fluellen for Llewellyn.

Forbes

It seems likely that this surname incorporates *fear*, 'man', and means 'man of property'. It is occasionally used as a first name for the first son of a woman whose maiden name was Forbes. According to Scottish tradition, the first Forbes was called Ochonochar and he settled in Scotland after killing a great bear.

Forgal(l)

Forgal was the father of Emer, who

was sought after by Cúchulainn. Forgal sent his future son-in-law to Scotland to train as a champion so that he might be worthy of Emer. The name may be a variant of Fergal or *fear(r)* + *gal* and mean 'brave, courageous man'.

Fransez
SEE: **Fanch**

Fraoch
Fraoch was a warrior and a contemporary of Cúchulainn. His name comes from *fraoch*, may mean 'heather', and is the equivalent of '-free' in Yeats's poem, *The Lake Isle of Innisfree*.

Fraser, Frazier, Frizzell
The Frasers were originally Normans from La Fraselière in France. The 'l' in the name accounts for the fact that the Frasers were called *Friseal* in Gaelic, a name that can mean 'fresh'. The chief of the Fraser clan is called *Mac Shimi*, son of Simon, because Simon Fraser was executed in 1747 for the support he gave to Bonnie Prince Charlie.

Fyfe
SEE: **Fife**

Fymber
SEE: **Finbar**

Gabhan, Gowan (pronounced like 'gow + an'), Gowon
Gabhan comes from Gaelic *gabha*,

'smith', and is found in the surnames Gowan and McGowan. Smiths were highly prized in the past, especially in times of war.
SEE: **Gobnait(t)**

Gael (pronounced like 'gale')
Gael occurs as a first name in Brittany and probably comes from *gaedheal*, meaning 'Irish'. The variants Gail and Kelig are also found.

Gair (pronounced like 'gare')
Gair is occasionally found in Scotland. It was originally a nickname meaning 'short' coming from Gaelic *gearr*.

Galahad (pronounced like 'gal + a + had')
Galahad was the son of Lancelot and Alaine or Elaine, Lord Tennyson's the Lady of the Lake. Although his parents were not married, he was the purest and gentlest knight ever to have lived. He spent his life searching for the Holy Grail, believed to be the chalice used by Christ at the Last Supper. His name may be a form of the Hebrew Gil(e)ad or he may have been called after his father's friend Galahaut, which probably comes from *Gaul* + *haut*, means 'tall Frenchman'.

Galahaut (pronounced like 'gal + a + ( )hote')
Galahaut was a close friend of Lancelot's. He knew about the love affair between Guinevere and his

friend and helped them to keep their secret. His name may be French and mean 'tall Gaul', from *Gaul* + *haut*. According to tradition, Lancelot was French and his brother also had 'Gal-' in his name. He was Galehodin.

Galaher, Gallagher, Gallaher

(pronounced like 'gal + a + her') These names all come from Gaelic *gall*, 'foreign' + *cabhair*, 'help' and mean 'foreign help'. They are attractive and resemble Galahad in form.

Gall (pronounced like 'gawl')

SEE: **Goll**

Galvin

Galvin may come from *geal* + *finn* or *fionn* and mean 'very white, fair' or it may be a form of 'sparrow' from Gaelic *gealbhán*. Sparrow was an appropriate nickname for an Irish saint because of the bird's use in religious writings. Psalm 84 points out that sparrows find a home on the Lord's altar.

> Yea, the sparrow hath found a house...
>
> (Psalm 84)

and Christ stressed the value of every human being, of whatever rank:

> Are not five sparrows sold for two farthings, and not one of them is forgotten before God?
> Even the very hairs of your head are all numbered. Fear not, therefore, ye are of more value than many sparrows.
>
> (Luke, 12: 6-7)

Gannon

Gannon was a Tyrone leader after whom the town of Dungannon (Gannon's fort) is called. The name may mean 'little loved one' if we relate Gannon to *gean*, 'love, affection'. Gannon can be a surname, but it has been used as a first name by Dungannon people living abroad.

Garbhán (pronounced like 'gar + van'), Garvin, Gervan, Gervin, Girvin, Gurvan

Garbhán was a popular Irish name and so it was quite widely adopted as a surname. It comes from *garbh*, 'rough to the touch' and means 'rugged'. Variants are now found in many parts of the world although the Gurvan form seems to be confined to Brittany.

Gareth (pronounced like 'ga + rith')

Gareth is often thought to be a Welsh form of Gerald and it may certainly have been influenced by the Norman use of Gerald. However, it seems to come from Welsh *gwared*, meaning 'gentle'.

Garret(t), Gearóid (pronounced like 'gar + ret', 'gar + rode'), Gerrit, Giraud

Gerald was introduced into the Celtic areas by the Normans. The name is related to Gerard, which comes from *gar* + *wald*, 'spear' + 'rule' and means 'noble warrior' or 'spear carrier'. Gareth is popular in Wales and Cornwall and is often regarded as being related to Garret or Garrett, which are frequently used in Ireland. All of them can be abbreviated to Gar, Gary or Garry. The forms Gerrit and Giraud have been recorded in Brittany.

Garvey, Garvie

These occur most frequently as a surname. They come from Gaelic *garbh* and mean 'rough peace' or 'peace after struggle'.

Garvin
SEE: Garbhán

Gavin, Gawain, Gawayne (pronounced like 'ga + vin' and 'ga + wane')

These names are related. Gavin is now found in Ireland, Scotland and the Isle of Man. The forms with 'w' were used mainly in the Cornwall–Wales region. They both probably come from *gwalch + gwyn*, meaning 'white hawk of battle'. An indication of the links between the Celtic communities is suggested by the fact that King Arthur's nephew and heir was Gawain of Orkney. His power as a warrior grew until the sun was at its highest and then diminished as the sun went down. The last great alliterative poem written in English was the fourteenth-century *Gawain and the Green Knight* and, although the poem is in English, many of the motifs are Celtic.

Gearóid
SEE: Garrett

Geraint, Gereint, Gerent (pronounced like 'ge + raint' and 'ge + rent')

Geraint is now the usual Welsh spelling but the form Gerent is recorded for Cornwall and the story of Gereint and Enid is a popular Arthurian legend. It is likely that all these forms are related to Greek *Gerontios*, which comes from *geron*, 'old man'. (One should remember that age was revered in the past and so this name was a term of respect.) St Gerent was honoured with a church in tenth-century Cornwall and with another in Dol, in Brittany.
SEE: Enid

Gerrit (pronounced like 'zher + eet')
SEE: Garret

Gervan, Gervin
SEE: Garbhán

Gerwyn (pronounced like 'ger + win')

This Welsh name looks like Gervin but it is, in fact, unrelated. It means 'fair love' and, although not yet as popular as some Welsh names, this one is likely to be widely used.

Gethen, Gethin (pronounced like 'geth + in')

Gethen comes from a Welsh *cethin*, meaning 'swarthy' or 'fierce'. It was originally a nickname but has become a name in its own right. Occasionally, this name is also given to a dark-haired, dark-eyed girl.

Gildas, Gweltaz (pronounced like 'gil + das' and 'gwel + tez')

Gildas is used in both Wales and Brittany. It is possible that the name comes from French Giles, which was taken from Greek *aigidion*, 'kid'. We know that Giles and Gyles were and are popular in the Cornish area, where the eighth-century Greek saint Giles was adulated. Gildas has the pet form Gweltaz in Brittany.

Gilroy

Gilroy is less well-known than Kilroy but it is attractive in both form and meaning. It probably comes from a blend of Gaelic *giolla*, 'devoted follower or servant' and French *roi*, 'king'. The 'king' could also be Christ, or '-roy' could be from the Gaelic word *ruadh*, 'red-headed'

Giraud
SEE: Garret

Girvin
See: Garbhán

Glen, Glenn, Glyn

The Hollywood star Glenn Ford made this name popular. It comes from Gaelic *gleann*, 'valley', and is used also as a surname. Welsh *glyn* also means 'valley' and is used as a first name.

Glendon

Glendon comes from Gaelic *gleann*, 'valley, glen', plus *dún*, fortress, and so implies 'one from the fortress in the glen'.

Glyn

The Celtic words for 'valley' are all similar. *Glyn* is the Welsh form and it has become a popular name in Wales and in Welsh-influenced communities throughout the world. Occasionally, it is used as an abbreviation for the famous Welsh patriot, Glyndwr.
SEE: Glen

Glyndwr (pronounced like 'glin + dhuer' or 'glen + dower')

Glyndwr is from Welsh *glyn* + *du*, 'black valley'. It was the name of the Welsh patriot Owain Glyndwr or Owen Glendower, 1359-1416. He led a successful revolt against the English in North Wales and defeated Henry IV in three campaigns between 1400 and 1402.

Goibhniú
SEE: Gabhan

Goll, Gall

Goll, or less frequently Gall, was a king in third-century Ireland. His name may be from gall, meaning 'foreigner, stranger'. Yeats has immortalised him in a poem called 'The Madness of King Goll'. According to legend, Goll fought bravely but went mad after seeing the pain and suffering that war could bring. Perhaps, in today's world, Goll's 'madness' might be regarded as sanity.

Gordon

Gordon is, in fact, probably an

English name meaning 'corner + hill'. It is now the name of a Scottish clan whose chief is known as 'The Cock o' the North', and it is popular worldwide, especially among people with a Scottish connection.

Gorman, Gormley

Gorman may come from the Gaelic adjective *gorm*, 'blue, noble', and thus Gormley would mean 'blue-eyed little one' or 'noble warrior. (The Picts were supposed to paint themselves blue before going into battle.) This name, like so many Celtic names, has gone from given name to surname and back again to given name.

Gowon
SEE: Gabhan

Grady

Grady and O'Grady are probably from Gaelic *gradaim*, 'distinction, honour'. They are almost exclusively surnames in Ireland but both have been used as given names in America.

Graeme
SEE: Graham

Graham, Grahame, Graeme

Graham is thought of as quintessentially Scottish but the name comes from Old English *grand*, 'gravel' + *ham*, 'settlement', and is actually the same name as Grantham, the town of Margaret Thatcher's birth. The Scots Gaelic form of the name is *Greumach* and the motto of the Graham clan is *Ne oublie*, 'don't forget'.

Grant

Grant is closely associated with Scotland but it comes from French *grand*, 'big', and was used by the Normans when they settled in Celtic communities. Grant is used in America by people of Scottish origin and also by people who want to honour the memory of US President Ulysses S. Grant.

Gregor

Gregor is experiencing renewed popularity in both Ireland and Scotland. The name comes from Gregory, which was originally from Greek *gregorios*, 'watchful'. It is best known, perhaps, in the clan name MacGregor but it is an attractive alternative to Gregory.

Griffith, Gryffydd (pronounced like 'grif + ith' and 'grif + fidh')

It is not clear where the Welsh name Griffith comes from, although it is suggested that it is a form of *rufus*, meaning 'red-haired'. Rufus is Latin but it was the nickname of William the Conqueror's son, William Rufus.

Guaire (pronounced like 'gwy + ir + ih'), Guerar (pronounced like 'gair + are'), Gwair

These names are probably related, although the first is found in Ireland, the second in Cornwall and the third in Wales. Guaire was a sixth-century

Irish king who lived at Gort in Galway. Guerar was a saint who was buried at St Neot in Cornwall. Gwair is a character in Welsh legends. The meaning of the name is disputed, but Guaire may be related to *gáire* and so mean 'laugh, good cheer'.

Gurvan
SEE: **Garbhán**

Guthrie
Guthrie occurs occasionally in Scotland and the north of Ireland. It probably means 'war hero' or the first syllable may be from Gaelic *gaoth*, 'breeze'.

Gwair
SEE: **Guaire**

Gweltaz
SEE: **Gildas**

Gwennin, Gwyn
These names probably both derive from a Celtic word *gwyn*, 'white, fair, pure'. Gwennin is still used in Brittany and Gwyn is becoming popular in Wales.

Gwilherm, Gwilym (pronounced like 'gwil + erm' and 'gwil + lim')
Both of these names are versions of William, which was originally Germanic and came from *will*, 'will' + *helm*, 'helmet'. The Breton form Gwilherm and the Welsh variant Gwilym seem to date back to the period of William the Conqueror, who was called Guillaume in French.
SEE: **Liam**

Gwyn
SEE: **Gwennin**

Gwynfor (pronounced like 'gwin + vor')
Gwynfor comes from Welsh *gwyn*, 'white, fair' + *ior*, 'lord', and, like many Welsh names, is more popular now than at any time in the past.
SEE: **Wynford**

Habloc (pronounced like 'hab + lock')
SEE: **Abloec**

Haco (pronounced like 'hack + o' or 'hay + co')
We do not know what Haco's name means but it may be related to *aodh*, 'flame, fire'. We also know that he was a Cornish leader who was betrothed to a beautiful princess. The Dane, Sigtryg, wanted the princess for himself and so dressed up as a minstrel and attended the wedding ceremony. Haco was so impressed by the beauty of Sigtryg's music and the anticipated pleasure of his bride that he rashly offered Sigtryg any wish. Sigtryg wished, of course, for the princess.

Hagan (pronounced like 'hay + gan')
Hagan is a modified form of Egan, meaning 'little fire'.
SEE: **Egan**

Hamish (pronounced like 'hay + mish')
Hamish is a Scottish form of Seamus or

Seumas. All Celtic names had vocative forms, that is forms used in address. Thus, a boy might be called Seamus, but he would be addressed as A Sheamuis and this would be pronounced like 'a hyamish'. Hamish is thus a form of James, which means 'heel'.

SEE: **Seamus**

Harvey, Herve, Herveig (pronounced like 'har + vee' and 'air + vay')

Harvey is thought to be of Breton origin and to mean 'worthy in battle'. The variant Herve is becoming popular again in France.

Hearn, Hearne
SEE: **Allan**

Heddwyn (pronounced like 'hed + win')

Heddwyn looks Welsh and is certainly found in Wales, where it is interpreted as 'holy peace'. Certainly *heddwch* is 'peace' and *gwynfydedig* is 'holy, blessed'. It is also possible that it is a Welsh form of Edwin, meaning 'friend of fortune'. Either way, it is an attractive name.

Herve, Hervey
SEE: **Harvey**

Hogan

Hogan may be a form of Hagan or it may be from Gaelic *ógán*, meaning 'youth'. It is most frequently used as a surname but has occurred as a given name, particularly when it is a mother's maiden name.

Howell (pronounced like 'how + ell')
SEE: **Hywel**

Hugh, Huw, Kew (pronounced like 'hyoo' and 'kyoo')

Hugh, its Welsh equivalent, Huw, and probably the Cornish Kew, are from a Germanic word *hug*, meaning 'heart, mind, spirit' and the same name is found in Hubert, from *hug* + *berht*, 'bright spirit' and, indeed, in the surname Hughes, which is an alternative spelling of Hugh's. Hugh was often used as a translation of Aodh in Ireland and the name has been popular among poets, patriots and saints. The form Hugo is a latinised form of Hugh, although it is often thought of as a separate name.

SEE: **Aodh**

Hywel (pronounced like 'how + ell')

Hywel is a Welsh name that means 'eminent'. This name has given rise to the surname Powell, which comes from *ap* + *Hywel*, 'son of Hywel'. Howell is an anglicised form of Hywel.

Iagan
SEE: **Egan**

Ian, Iain, Ieuan, Iwan (pronounced like 'ee + an' and 'yew + an')

Ian and Iain are Scottish forms of John and thus mean 'God is gracious'. The forms Ian and Iain are found in many communities as well as Scotland, while the forms Ieuan and Iwan are found mainly in Wales.

SEE: **Evan**

Iarnan

SEE: **Ernan**

Idris (pronounced like 'ee + driss' or 'eye + driss')

Idris comes from Welsh *iud*, 'lord' + *ris*, 'fiery, ardent'. It was used in the Middle Ages but then, like many Welsh names, virtually died out, only to be reinstated as a popular name in the nineteenth and twentieth centuries.

Idwal (pronounced like 'eed + wal' or 'yood + wal')

Idwal comes from *iud*, 'lord' and means 'lord' or 'rampart lord'. It is less widely used than many Welsh names but may become more popular.

Ieuan

SEE: **Ian**

Ifor, Ivor

Ifor is a Welsh form of the Scandinavian name Ivor, from *yr* + *herr*, 'yew + army', which means 'archer'. One of the best-known characters to bear this name is the Welsh-sounding cartoon character, Ivor the Engine.

Illtud, Illtyd (pronounced like 'ill + tood')

Illtud's name probably comes from Welsh *iud*, 'lord' and means 'lord of all'. He was King Arthur's cousin and was believed to be the most learned man alive. He was born in Brittany, where his feast day is still celebrated on 6 November, but founded an Abbey in Wales, where he was known as Illtyd.

Inir, Ynyr (pronounced like 'in + eer')

Inir is a lovely Welsh name, coming from *ynyr*, meaning 'honour'. It has been underused in the past but may become popular. The female forms Inira, Inire and Ynyra have been used as Welsh equivalents of the Latin-inspired Honora.

Innes, Innis (pronounced like 'in + iss')

Innis is used as a clan name and a given name in Scotland. The clan name may come from *innis*, 'island', and Malcolm IV gave the Innis lands to Beorwald from Flanders in 1160. The given name may also be a form of Aengus. MacInnis is sometimes a form of Mac Aongusa.

Iobhar, Ivi (pronounced like 'yo + var' and 'ee + vee')

The Gaelic word *iobhar* or *iúr* means 'yew'. Versions of this name are found in all Celtic languages because it derives from the name of the yew tree. Trees were significant to the Celts and circles of hawthorn, oak or yew trees had mystical significance for the druids. Of course, we cannot be absolutely certain that our ancestors used the same name for the same tree. All the Indo-European languages have related words: Old High German had *iwa*; Old Norse had *yr*; Latin had *uva* but it referred to the 'grape'; and Russian has *iva* but it means 'willow'. The form Ivi was found in Cornwall and is still used in Brittany, where the feast of Saint Ivi is celebrated on 6 October.

Iollan, Yollan, Yolland (pronounced like 'yoll + an(d)')

Iollan was the son of Fergal and a champion at the court of Conchubhar. He went to Scotland to persuade Deirdre and the sons of Usna to return home. He believed that Conchubhar had forgiven them. When he returned with them and discovered his mistake, he died defending them. It is not certain what Iollan's name comes from although it may be linked to *íol*, 'one who worships a different god'. In his play, *Translations*, Brian Friel gives the name Yolland to a young English soldier, who falls in love with Máire and with Irish culture.

Iorweth, Yorath (pronounced like 'yor + ith')

Iorweth occurs in Wales and comes from *ior*, meaning 'lord'. It is found most frequently as a surname.

Iorwyn, Yorwin, Yorwyn (pronounced like 'yor + win')

Iorwyn comes from *ior* + *gwyn* and means 'pure or handsome lord'. It is an attractive name but not widely used.

Ith (pronounced like 'eeh')

This unusual name belonged to a Milesian, a son of Milesius, a king of Spain whose sons were said to have conquered Ireland. Ith was the first of the Gaels to die on Irish soil. The meaning of his name is uncertain but it may be related to *iocht*, 'kindness, mercy'.

Ithel (pronounced like 'eeth + el')

Ithel is not, apparently, related to Irish Ith. It seems to come from *ior* + *hael*, meaning 'generous lord' and is one of the many Welsh names currently being used for the first time in centuries.

Iuchar, Iucharba (pronounced like 'yuch + are' and 'yuch + are + ba')

Iuchar, Iucharba and Brian were sons of Tuireann and their story has probably changed greatly over the centuries. The brothers were responsible for curtailing the activities of Cian, who could change himself into any shape in order to avoid capture. According to one legend, the brothers trapped him when he was in the body of a pig. When they buried him, however, Cian was able to dig a trench and escape. The meaning of Iuchar and Iucharba is uncertain but they may be related to *íocóir*, *'one who pays'*.

Ivi
SEE: **Iobhar**

Ivor
SEE: **Ifor**

Iwan
SEE: **Ian**

J

Jago, Jagu, Jegu, Jacut (pronounced like 'jay + go' and 'ya + go')
Jago is a Cornish form of Jacob, a Hebrew name which was also anglicised as James. The biblical Jacob was the son of Rebecca and Isaac and the twin brother of Esau. He is said to have held on to his brother's heel when he was born, and so the name may mean 'heel' or it may mean 'supplanter' because Jacob supplanted his brother as Isaac's heir. The Cornish name is pronounced like 'jay + go'. The other three forms are Breton, underlining the link between Breton and Cornish. The 'j' tends to be pronounced like 'zh' in Brittany, under the influence of French.

Jakez (pronounced like 'zhak', 'jake' or 'jakes')
Although Jakez is a Breton form of Jacques, the French form of James, it is often regarded as a separate name.
SEE: **Jago, Seamus**

Jared, Jarret (pronounced like 'jar + red' or 'ja + ret')
Jared and Jar(r)et are related to Gareth and Garrett and come from Germanic, *gar + hard*, which means 'hardy spear (carrier)'. They are both used, especially in Ireland, where they have possibly been influenced by the name of a sixth-century saint, Iarlath or Jarlath.
SEE: **Gareth**

Jegu
SEE: **Jago**

Job, Jos
Job and Jos are used in Brittany as forms of Joseph, a name that means 'God shall add'. It occurs frequently in the Bible and was the name of the son of Jacob who held an important post in Egypt. It was also the name of the carpenter foster father of Jesus. Job and Jos are associated with St Joseph the Worker.
SEE: **Seosamh**

Jonty
This is sometimes used as an anglicised form of Seantaigh, 'little John'.
SEE: **Seán**

Ka, Kai, Kay, Key (pronounced like 'key')
It is possible that Kay comes from Gaelic *caoi*, meaning 'path, way', but it is more likely that it comes from Welsh and means 'field of battle'. This was the name of one of King Arthur's knights but it is now thought of exclusively as a girl's name.
SEE: **Cai**

Kadec, Kadeg
SEE: **Caddock**

Kane, Kain
Kane may come from *cian*, 'dark one' or from the old Irish name Cathán, meaning 'war champion'.
SEE: **Cian**

Karantec, Karantoc
SEE: **Carannog**

Karl
SEE: **Carroll**

Kary
This is a variant spelling of Carey, related to Welsh *car*, 'beloved'.
SEE: **Carey**

Kean(e)
Kean is probably based on the Irish surname Kean(e) but it could also be a modern spelling of *cian*, meaning 'ancient' or 'long-lasting'.
SEE: **Cian**

Kearney
SEE: **Carney**

Keegan
This name comes from a wrong division of MacEgan, becoming MaKeegan and eventually Keegan. It means 'son of the little fire'.
SEE: **Egan**

Keelan
In theory, Keelan, which comes from *caoil* + *finn* or *fionn* means 'slender and fair', could be used equally for boys and girls. In practice, it is more widely used for girls.
SEE: **Caoilfhinn**

Keeley
Keeley probably comes from cadhla, a poetic name for 'beautiful'. This surname has followed the route of many others. It has been used first as a name for boys and has then become more widely used as a name for girls.

Keenan
Keenan, the surname, comes from a diminutive of *cian* and thus means 'little ancient one', a name that some- times suggested a reincarnated person. In Irish tradition, reincarn- ation was not a fate to be avoided, as it is in Hinduism, but one to be sought after.
SEE: **Cian**

Keir
Keir is a Scottish surname that was popularised as a first name by the politician, Keir Hardie. The name probably comes from *ciar*, meaning 'dark haired'.

Keiron
SEE: **Ciarán**

Keith
Keith was originally Scottish and probably came from a form of *coillte* or *ceiteach*, meaning 'woods'. It has moved far from Scotland and is now used worldwide. It is possible that Keith was influenced also by Welsh *coedwig*, 'forest', and even by Old English *cuth*, 'knowledgeable'.

Keller
There is still considerable debate about the origins of this name but it seems likely that it is related to Gaelic *ceilidh(e)*, 'get together', and could thus mean 'companion'.

Kelly
Kelly is one of the commonest surnames in Ireland and is also found

widely in the Isle of Man. It was originally a man's name, possibly from *ceallach*, meaning 'hermit', but is almost exclusively used for girls now.

Kelvin

Strange as it may sound – and truth is often stranger than fiction – Kelvin is a Scottish name derived from the River Clyde, and Glasgow has an area, Kelvinside, named after it. The form of the name has been influenced by Melvin, and it has become popular worldwide.

Kendrick

Kendrick, like many old names, has at least two possible derivations. It may come from the wrong division of Scottish MacEanruigh, 'son of Henry', 'son of home power', or it may come from Old English words meaning 'keen power'. The fact that the name occurs much more widely in Scotland than elsewhere suggests that the Gaelic meaning may be the older one.

Kenn

Kenn is occasionally used, especially in America. It may be an abbreviation of Kenneth, meaning 'born of fire', or it may be a variant of *cion*, 'love, affection'. Either way, it is attractive both as a reduced form and as a name in its own right.

Kennedy

This surname originated in Ireland and Scotland and probably comes from *ceann éitigh*, 'ugly head', although some Kennedys suggest that it really means 'helmeted head'. The use of Kennedy as a first name owes much to the respect that was felt for John F. Kennedy, the assassinated President of the United States.

Kenneth

Kenneth almost certainly comes from Scots Gaelic *coinneach*, 'born of fire'. One of the earliest Kenneths was a sixth-century Irish saint who left his monastery after it was ravaged by plague. He spent time in both Wales and Scotland and many legends grew up around him.

SEE: **Canice**

Kent

Kent comes from the name of an English county but the name of the county is almost certainly from an old Celtic word meaning 'border' and is possibly related to Welsh *cenedl*, 'nation'. Kent is also used as an abbreviated form of Kentigern.

Kentigern (pronounced like 'kent + ig + earn')

Kentigern, who is also known as Mungo, was the son of a Pictish princess. When it was discovered that she was pregnant, she was condemned to be thrown off a high cliff, but God miraculously intervened and she was set adrift in a coracle without a sail or an oar. The coracle drifted to the Fife coast, where she was looked after by St Serf. He baptised her and the son that she gave birth to and he called the boy Kentigern, a name that may be related to *ciontaigh* and thus mean 'I do not condemn you'. Serf grew to love the boy so much that he called him Mungo or 'greatly loved'. The boy grew up to be bishop of Glasgow, and his fame spread throughout Europe so that the name Kentigern is still used in Brittany, where his feast day is celebrated on 14 March.

Kermit, Kermode

Like many names that begin with 'k' or 'q', these are forms of MacDermot or MacDiarmaid that were pronounced MacErmot or MacIarmuid and then divided in the wrong place. They both mean 'son of the free man' or 'son of the one without envy'. Kermit is probably no longer acceptable as a boy's name because of the success of Kermit the frog in *The Muppet Show* but Kermode is an attractive alternative.
SEE: **Dermot**

Kerry

Kerry probably comes from Co Kerry and was once more frequently used for a boy than a girl. Today, however, it is almost invariably a girl's name.
SEE: **Ceri, Kerry**

Keverne, Kevin, Kevan

These are both forms of Irish *Caoimhín*, meaning 'handsome and well born'. Kevern(e) is the Cornish form and it is still found in the placename St Keverne. Kevin is found almost everywhere else,

although Kevan has also been used. The form Kevin is used in Brittany, as are the variants Gavin and Coemgen.
SEE: **Caoimhghín**

Kew

SEE: **Hugh**

Key

Key is an alternative spelling for Kay or Cai. One of the Knights of the Round Table was called Sir Kay but it is also possible that Key comes from McKee, 'son of Aodh' or 'son of fire'.
SEE: **Cai, Kay**

Kieran, Kieron

Kieran is a very popular Irish name from *ciar*, meaning 'dark one'. It is found in Brittany, where St Kieran's feast day is still celebrated on 5 March. One of the earliest Kierans on record was made a bishop by St Patrick and thus the name goes back to the fifth century at least.
SEE: **Ciarán**

Killian

Killian is popular worldwide and, due to the influence of Irish missionaries, it is quite widely used in Cameroon and Nigeria. The name is likely to come from *cill*, 'church', but it may also mean 'struggle'. Irish missionary saints called Killian took the name to France and the form Kilian is still found in Brittany.
SEE: **Cillian**

Kinnell

Kinnell is a fairly rare surname. The name may come from *cineál*, 'kindness', in which case it could be an attractive name for either a boy or a girl. In rural parts of Northern Ireland the word 'kinnel' is used for a warm drink that is given to an animal that has just given birth.

Kinnock
SEE: **Canank**

Kolman
SEE: **Colm**

Konan
SEE: **Conan**

Kyle
Kyle, which may come from cill, 'church', is most frequently used in Scotland, where it is taken from the region that is now in Strathclyde.

Kynon
Kynon is a Welsh and Cornish form of Conan, which may mean 'highly intelligent'. The form Konan is found in Brittany.
SEE: **Conan**

Labhras (pronounced like 'lau + russ' or 'low + russ')
Labhras is an Irish form of Laurence, which was based on a Roman place name, Laurentum, although it was probably influenced by *laurus*, 'laurel wreath', a symbol of high success. There have been several saints called Laurence but the best-known one is the third-century martyr. In recent memory, people in

Ireland often associated their suffering with the suffering of Labhras by saying: 'Labhras, burned on a gridiron, pray for us'.

Labraid (pronounced like 'lab + ridge' or 'lav + ridge')
Labraid seems to have been a popular name in the past. Because it is such an old name, its meaning is unclear but it may be related to *labhairt*, 'speech'. Labraid was a king of the other world where Irish gods and immortals lived. When it looked as if he was losing control of his kingdom, he sent his wife to get Cúchulainn's help. Labraid was also the name of a Leinster king who had long ears. He hid these from everyone but his barber, who was under strict instructions not to tell a living person. The barber finally unburdened himself to a tree, but when the tree was cut down and turned into a harp, the harp immediately sang out the story of Labraid's long ears.

Lach, Lachlan, Lachlann, Lochlann (pronounced like 'loch' and 'loch + lan')
Lachlann is used almost exclusively in Scotland. It means 'Viking, stranger from the land of the lochs', this being a shorter version of Maoilsheachlainn. It sometimes occurs in the surname Loughlan or Loughlin.

Lance, Lancelot, Launcelot
Lancelot's name is one of the best known in Celtic legends. It is not

certain what his name means. It has been suggested that it comes from French *lance* and means 'spear carrier', but it is more likely that it was originally a Celtic name connected with *llan*, 'church'. Lancelot was, indeed, very devout and is believed to have raised a knight from the dead by the strength of his prayer. Lancelot had only one flaw: he could not overcome his love for Guinevere, Arthur's wife. The abbreviated form Lance is currently very popular.

Lann

This Gaelic name comes from *lann*, 'sword'. It is not widely used but is an attractive alternative to Lance.

Lanval (pronounced like 'lan + val')

Lanval's name may have come from *llan + uchel*, 'high church'. He was a Knight of the Round Table who married an immortal woman. She was everything that a man could hope for but she could only stay with him if her origins were kept secret. Lanval boasted about her, and when he returned home she had disappeared.

Laoghaire

SEE: **Loegaire**

Lear, Lir (pronounced like 'leer')

It is possible that Lear's name comes from a Celtic adjective such as *liath*, meaning 'grey' and implying that he deserved respect. The name is attractive in both forms, but it is unlikely to be popular because of its associations with tragedy: Lear was

the father of four children who were turned into swans. He is father of the sea god Manannan and his name also means 'sea'.

SEE: **Fionnuala**

Leary

SEE: **Loegaire**

Lee, Leigh

Lee may have several origins. It may come from Old English *leah*, 'wood'; it may come from Welsh *lle*, 'place'; it may come from the River Lee in Ireland; or from Gaelic *laoi*, 'poem, lay'. Whatever, its origin or origins, it is currently popular and the Lee form is also used for girls.

Lennon

Lennon is a popular Irish surname, possibly from *léana* meaning 'meadow'. It started being used as a first name after the death of the Beatle, John Lennon in 1980.

Lennox

Lennox is a surname in Scotland. It was originally a placename and probably came from *leamhán*, 'elm' and meant 'grove of elms'. It has become popular as a first name in Caribbean families. The fame and good looks of world heavyweight boxer, Lennox Lewis, will guarantee that it remains a popular choice.

Leslie

SEE: **Lesley**

Liam

Liam is the Irish form of William.

William was originally a Germanic name, *wil(l)* + *helm*, meaning 'will + helmet' and probably suggesting 'strong protection'. The Normans took the name to England in 1066 in the form of Guillaume, and Liam is probably an Irish version of this, rather than the second half of William. Like Barry, Kevin and Sean, this name is currently very popular in England, even in families with no Irish connection.

SEE: **Gwilherm**

Lir
SEE: **Lear**

Lleufer (pronounced like 'hloo + ver')
Lleufer is Welsh and means 'splendid'. It is perhaps less popular than it deserves to be because many people have difficulty spelling and pronouncing it.

Llew (pronounced like 'hloo' or 'loo')
Llew seems to mean 'radiant light' although it is also the Welsh word for 'lion'. It may be based on a Celtic sun god, identical to Irish Lugh. Certainly, the stories told about them are similar. Llew was renowned for his skill with weapons and was sometimes called Llew Llaw Gyffes, or Llew of the Skilful Hand. The Irish Lugh was called Lugh of the Long Hand. (The Celts used the same word for 'hand' and 'arm'.)

Llewellyn, Llywelyn, Llew (pronounced like 'hloo + ell + in')
Llewellyn is the slightly anglicised form of a Welsh name, Llywelyn, that was borne by a Welsh prince, Llywelyn ap Iorweth, in the twelfth century. Its meaning is uncertain but it is claimed to include *llew*, 'lion' and mean 'lion-like, mighty ruler'. This name, more than many others, immediately conjures up Welshness.

Lloyd (pronounced like 'hloid' or 'loid')
Lloyd comes from the Welsh adjective *llwyd*, meaning 'grey' and suggesting 'grey-haired, mature'. It has also been anglicised as Floyd, because English people found it hard to begin a name with the Welsh sound represented by 'll'. (A good way to pronounce it is to put 'h' in front of the 'l' and so say 'hloid'. This is not perfect, but it is a step in the right direction.)

Llywelyn
SEE: **Llewellyn**

Lochinvar (pronounced like 'loch + in + var')
Lochinvar was the hero in a poem by Sir Walter Scott:

O, young Lochinvar is come out
of the west,
Through all the wide Border his
steed was the best.

His name may mean 'inlet Viking' or 'Viking of Inver' .

SEE: **Lachlann**

Lochlan(n)
This is the Irish form of a name that meant 'Viking'. It was given to boys

who had fair or red hair.
SEE: **Lachlann**

Loegaire (pronounced like 'lug + oy + ir + ih')

It is not certain what this name means although it may be related to *log + gaire*, 'place of laughter, joy'. Loegaire was a charioteer and friend of Cúchulainn. He married a beautiful immortal who took him to the Land of Eternal Youth. For a while he was happy but then longed to see his home again. His wife gave him a horse and told him not to dismount. When Loegaire went back, he found that hundreds of years had passed and that the great halls of Conchubhar were in ruins. He got off the horse to lament the passing of a way of life but, as soon as his foot touched the ground, he grew old and joined his former companions in death.

Loeiz, Loic, Loig (pronounced like 'loo + eece' or 'loo + eek')

These are Breton forms of Louis, a name that was originally Germanic *hlod + wig*, 'fame + war' and meant 'famous in war'. It was the most frequently used king's name in France from the Middle Ages until the French Revolution.

Logan

Logan is a surname in Scotland and Ireland and probably comes from a placename, *logán*, meaning 'hollow'. It has begun to be used as a first name, possibly under the influence of the popular Rogan.

Loic, Loig
SEE: **Loeiz**

Lorcan, Lorcán

The Gaelic word *lorc* means 'fierce' and the name was probably a nickname for a brave warrior. It is an extremely attractive name and, although it is sometimes equated with Laurence, it is a name in its own right and one that is growing in popularity.

Lugh (pronounced like 'Lou')

Lugh is related to Gaelic *luisne*, 'glow of light' and means 'shining light'. He was, as we might expect, a god and thus qualified to perform any task. The Celts seem to have worshipped a sun god, whose name began with 'L-'. Relics of places sacred to him include Lyons in France and Leeds in England.
SEE: **Llew**

Lughaidh (pronounced like 'loo + ee')

Lughaidh's name is based on Lugh and thus probably means 'carrier of light'. Lughaidh has the dubious fame of having defeated Cúchulainn in single combat. However, even the sword he used to behead the great warrior objected and cut off Lughaidh's own hand.

Macaulay, Macauley

Macaulay comes from *mac + amhlach*, 'son of the phantom'. It has been popularised as a first name by the Hollywood actor, Macaulay Culkin, best known, perhaps, for his roles in the *Home Alone* films.

Mackenzie, Mack

Mackenzie has become popular as a first name in Canada and America, largely among people of Scottish origin. The name means 'son of the bright one' and the Mackenzies have been a significant clan in Scotland for at least 700 years. One of the Mackenzies, the Earl of Seaforth, lost his estates for supporting James Stuart, the 'Old Pretender' in 1715, but his grandson worked hard and made enough shrewd investments to be able to buy back the land and titles in 1771.

Madeg, Madoc (pronounced like 'ma + deg' and 'ma + dock')

Madeg and Madoc are Breton forms of the Welsh name *Madoc*, meaning 'generous, forgiving'. They are also probably related to Malachy, which may come from *Mael + Madog*, 'follower of St Madog'. St Madog or Madoc was a seventh-century Irish monk revered throughout the Celtic, and indeed the Christian world, for his piety, austerity and devotion to the word of God. The Irish Madog is a pet form of Aodh, meaning 'fire', and may come from the phrase *mo Aodh óg*, meaning 'my young Aodh'.
SEE: **Madoc, Malachy**

Madoc (pronounced like 'ma + dock')

Madoc ap Owain Gwynedd was a legendary Welsh chieftain who is reputed to have discovered America in the twelfth century (a few centuries after St Brendan but three hundred years before Columbus!). It is hard to prove that Madoc did, in fact, visit the Americas although many writers have claimed to have found links between Europe and the Americas before Columbus visited the continent. Apparently, there are traces of tenth-century Cornish fishing villages in Newfoundland and genetic links between Native Americans of the Mid-West and the Welsh.

Mael, Malo, Mel

Mael, probably meaning 'devotee', is found in Brittany and has a feminine form Maela. It is possible that Malo, as in the port St Malo, is a related name. It is also possible that the saint who gave rise to the name was a devotee of St Andrew, the apostle and brother of Simon Peter. Mael's feast day is celebrated, like St Andrew, on 30 December.

Maeldún, Maelduine, Muldoon (pronounced like 'mwel + doon', 'mel + doon' and 'mull + doon')

Maeldún is an Irish traveller in the mould of St Brendan. His name may mean 'devotee of the dark warrior' or *dún* may refer to 'fortress'. He had a somewhat unusual background in that his mother was a nun and he was brought up by her friend, a princess. He set out to avenge his father's murder and found himself on a voyage of discovery, visiting islands where wonderful creatures lived and where vibrant, psychedelic colours predominated. One island had a population consisting only of women; another had treasure beyond the voyagers' dreams but the treasure was guarded by a cat! Paul Muldoon, the Irish poet, writes about Maeldún's *Immrama* and enjoys the Celtic joke of writing about oneself in the guise of writing about someone else.

Magee, McGee, McGhie

These names are all variants of *mach + Aodh*, 'son of fire'. The first is found as a surname in Northern Ireland, and in the island, Islandmagee; the second and third are found mainly in Scotland. Magee has begun to be used as a first name by people with the surname in their families.

Magnus, Manus (pronounced like 'man + us')

Manus, or less frequently Magnus, is used as a first name in Ireland. It comes originally from Latin *magnus*, 'big, great', and was popularised by Charlemagne, or Carolus Magnus, Charles the Great, who was crowned Roman Emperor in AD800. The name also occurs in the surname McManus. Ma(g)nus was popular throughout Europe. There was a Magnus who was the Earl of Orkney in the eleventh century and a Magnus Barefoot of Norway who invaded Orkney, displacing his namesake.

Mailyr (pronounced like 'mail + er')
SEE: **Meilyr**

Maines (pronounced like 'my + nus')

Maines may be a form of Magnus, 'great' or be related to *manach*, 'monk'. The poet, Yeats, writes about Maines, who was the son of Queen Madhbh. Maines had more courage than sense, perhaps, in that he engaged the great Cúchulainn in single combat, in an attempt to defend his mother's kingdom.

Malachy (pronounced like 'mal + a + kee')

Malachy comes from the Irish name *maoilsheachlainn*, and thus means 'follower or devotee of St Seachlainn'. The name was equated with the Hebrew prophet Malachi, whose name means 'messenger of God'. The name has been further popularised by Thomas Moore's melody 'The Minstrel Boy:

> When Malachy wore the collar of gold
> That he won from the proud invader.

Malcolm

Malcolm is one of the most popular Gaelic names. It comes from Gaelic *maol* (*mael*) + *colm* and means 'follower or devotee of the dove', where the 'dove' is usually St Columba. Many Gaelic names beginning with '*mal*' or '*mel*' can trace their origins to the fact that children were often dedicated to a saint or to Christ and called '*mal*' or '*gil*' + saint, as in Malcolm or Gilchrist.

SEE: **Colm**

Malo
SEE: **Mael**

Malvin
This may be the male equivalent of Malvina and mean 'devotee of Mena' or 'devotee of Finn'. It is also possible that it is a variant of Marvin, meaning 'sea fort'.

SEE: **Malvina, Marvin, Merlin**

Manannan, Manawyddan
Manannan, son of Lír, was an Irish god of the sea. His wife was Fand and he continued to love her even after she had had an affair with Cúchulainn. Manannan is associated with women in Irish tradition. He was the guardian of *Tír na mBan*, 'land of women', one of the Blessed Islands visited by Maeldun. The meaning of Manannan is uncertain but it may be related to the 'Man' in the Isle of Man. The Gaelic word for Manx is *Manainnis*. There is also a literary word *meanmanra*, meaning 'spirit, courage'. The Welsh equivalent is Manawyddan, regarded as being the son of Llyr and husband of Rhiannon.

Manus
SEE: **Magnus**

Maodez, Maudez, Mawes, Modez (pronounced like 'mo + days' and 'maws')
St Mawes is believed to have been born in Ireland but to have lived most of his life in Cornwall. He is reputed to have lived a holy and austere life, rarely opening his mouth to say anything but his prayers. Versions of his name are found also in Brittany, the most popular being Maodez. His feast day is celebrated on 18 November and his name may be related to Welsh *maddau*, 'forgive', an appropriate nickname for a bishop and confessor.

Maolíosa (pronounced like 'mwell + ee + sa')
This beautiful name has become popular for both boys and girls. It comes from *maol* + *Íosa*, meaning 'devotee of Jesus'. Some parents avoid using it for boys because the '-a' ending is so frequently associated with females in the rest of Europe.

Mark, Marrac (pronounced like 'mark' and 'mar + rack')
Mark was the king of Cornwall who planned to marry Isolt. At first, she was happy with the arrangement until she met Tristan. And the rest, as they say, is history. St Mark was an evangelist whose name seems to come from Latin *Marcus*, suggesting a follower of Mars and thus a warrior.

Marmaduke
Marmaduke sounds so English that it is hard to think of it as Celtic and yet it is an anglicisation of *mael*, 'devotee', + *Madoc*, 'generous'.

SEE: **Madoc**

Marrac
SEE: **Mark**

Marvin, Mervin, Morvan

Marvin comes from Welsh *Myrddyn*, meaning 'sea fort'. It is the same name as both Merlin and Mervin and all of them are anglicisations. The change from Marvin to Mervin is easy to explain. Many English words containg '-er-' were pronounced as if they were '-ar-', and so we have 'clerk' and 'Derby' (pronounced 'clark' and 'Darby'). Later, people used a spelling pronunciation and the first syllable of Mervin began to be rhymed with 'her' not 'tar'. The form Morvan is found in Brittany. This is an attractive variant and could also be seen as a blend of Mervin and Morgan.

SEE: **Merven, Morgan**

Math (pronounced like 'math')

Math was a great Welsh king, as renowned for his wisdom as Solomon. According to some traditions, he could only find happiness when his feet were in the lap of a virgin! It is possible that his name is related to Welsh *math*, 'sort, type'.

Maudez, Mawes
SEE: **Maodez**

Maxen

Maxen is a Welsh version of Magnus and thus means 'great'. It is an attractive name and is being used as a variant of Max, which comes from Latin Maximilian and means 'the greatest'.

SEE: **Magnus**

Maxwell

Maxwell is found as a surname in Scotland and means 'Manus's stream or water source' or 'Maccus's stream'. The surname was thus derived from a placename. Many Scottish Maxwells claim that they are descended from a King Maccus of the Isle of Man.

McGee, McGhie
SEE: **Magee**

Meilyr, Meilir, Melar, Melor
(pronounced like 'mail + er' and 'mel +or')

Meilyr is Welsh and means 'iron man'. It is not widely used but has appeared recently in these forms and, more rarely, as Mailyr. Melar and Melor are found in Brittany.

Mel
SEE: **Mael**

Melan, Mellanus (pronounced like 'mel + an' and 'mel + an + oos')

St Melan or Mellanus was honoured in Cornwall until the Reformation. Very little is known about him except that he was a Celt. He continues to be honoured in Brittany, where his feast day is celebrated on January 6, the Epiphany. It is an interesting speculation that his name implies that he was black or dark. Greek *melas* means 'black' and Christian tradition suggests that one of the Three Kings, who followed the Star of Bethlehem, was black.

Melor, Melorus, Mylor

Melor was probably a Breton saint, who continues to be honoured in Brittany, but some traditions suggest that he was the son of a Cornish king and a Devonian lady. It seems certain, however, that his relics were brought to Wiltshire probably around 979 and that he was patron saint of Mylor in Cornwall. We know that he was honoured throughout the Celtic world and the legends surrounding his life overlap with legends of Celtic heroes. His name may mean 'iron man', the same as Welsh, *Meilyr* or the 'Mel-' may suggest that he was a new devotee of a particular saint, since *úr* means 'new'. According to tradition, he lost a hand and a foot but clever smiths replaced both and his silver hand developed all the feelings and skills of a real hand.

SEE: **Nuada**

Melville, Melvin, Melvyn

These names are all derived from a Scottish placename, Malleville, a place settled by the Normans and named 'bad town', presumably because the land was infertile. Malleville became Melville and was adopted first as a surname and then, increasingly, as a given name. The change from Melville to Melvin was helped by the existence of other names ending in '-in', names such as Devlin, Kelvin, McEwin. The spelling with '-yn' was the result of fashion. Similar changes of spelling are found in Martyn and Gavyn.

Meriadeg, Meriadoc, Meredith

These names come from the given name *Maredudd* and mean 'great lord'. Meriadeg occurs in Brittany and the others mostly in Wales.

Merlin, Merlyn

Most people who know anything about King Arthur and the Knights of the Round Table have heard of Merlin, the sorcerer. His name comes from Welsh *Myrddyn*, meaning 'sea fort', a name that has also been anglicised as Marvin and Mervin. We owe the modern form of Merlin's name to Geoffrey of Monmouth's *Vita Merlini*, 'Life of Merlin'. Merlin was not just a magician. He was a poet, a prophet and a mystic. Arthur's defeat in battle was said to have made him mad, mad with sadness because their dreams of creating an earthly paradise were shattered by human weakness. There are many stories about Merlin's fate but one is particularly interesting. He was supposed to have been trapped in a tree by a woman to whom he told his secrets. In Shakespeare's *The Tempest*, Ariel was trapped in a tree by Caliban's mother. Perhaps Shakespeare owed more to Celtic sources than has hitherto been realised.

Merven, Mervin, Mervyn

It seems likely that Mervyn and its variants come from Welsh *merfyn*, supposedly from *mer*, 'marrow' +

ffynu, 'thriving'. Certainly, it was the name of a ninth-century Welsh king. Alternative origins suggest that Mervyn and Melvin are variants of Malvin and refer to a devotee of Mena, or of Merlin.

Miach (pronounced like 'mee + ach')
Miach was a skilled Irish craftsman, like his father Diancecht, who made a silver hand for Nuada. Miach discovered that he could create limbs from flesh and bone and may thus be the first transplant surgeon in the history of the world. His father was jealous of his son's skills and wounded Miach in the chest. Miach was, of course, able to heal the wound. The meaning of the name is uncertain but is possibly related to *miadh*, 'honour, distinction', and the existence of this name may have encouraged the popularity of Mícheál.

Mícheál (pronounced like 'me' + 'hall'), **Mikael**
Mícheál is an Irish form of Michael, a Hebrew name, meaning 'who is like God', and borne by the Archangel who cast Lucifer into Hell. Michael was often depicted as a soldier, bearing a sword of flame, and so was chosen as a role model for warriors. The name has lost much of its military association now and is more likely to be linked to one of the many singers or actors who have been called 'Michael'. The abbreviations Mick, Mickey, Mike and Mikey are also used in Ireland. The form Mikael is Breton and offers parents an attractive alternative.

Midhir (pronounced like 'me + dhir' or 'mee + ir')
We cannot be certain what Midhir's name means although it may be related to *míodhach*, 'healer'. He was King of the Sidhe and husband of Fuamnach who was punished by Aengus because of her treatment of Etain whom she changed into a fly.

Milo (pronounced like 'mile + o')
Anyone familiar with the theatre in Ireland will have heard of Milo O'Shea. It is possible that the name comes from Latin *milo*, a miller, or is an Irish form of Miles/Myles. There is a third possibility, that Milo is a shortened form of *maol* + *Muire*, meaning 'devotee of Mary'.

Mitchel, Mitchell, Mitch
Mitchell is a surname that is a variant of Michael and thus means 'who is like God'. It is popular, especially in America and has Mitch as an abbreviated form.

Modez (pronounced like 'mo + days' or 'mo + day')
SEE: **Maodez**

Moran, Moren, Muireann, Muirinn (pronounced like 'mor + an' or 'mwir + an')
These are forms of an Irish name *Muirinn*, meaning 'white as the sea'. It could be used of either sex, but the

closeness of the last two forms to Maureen tends to rule them out for boys in Ireland. Moran is also a widely-used surname in Ireland and a popular first name in Brittany.

Moray

Moray comes from a Scottish placename. Many Earls of Moray were regarded as being exceptionally handsome:

> He was the Earl o' Moray
> An' he played at the ba'
> An' the bonnie Earl o' Moray
> Was the best o' them a'.

SEE: **Muireachadh, Murray**

Moren

SEE: **Moran**

Morgan

Morgan can be linked to both Irish and Welsh and may mean either 'great queen' or 'bright sea, sea born'. The modern Irish word *móraigeanta*, 'magnanimous', is related. It is quite commonly used in both countries as a surname and the male name Morgan comes from the tradition of calling boys by surnames.

Morvan, Morven

These variants probably come from Gaelic *mór* + *finn*, meaning 'great fair one' and were probably originally used of a Viking invader. They are now more widely found as surnames than first names, although that could change quite quickly.

SEE: **Marvin**

Muireachadh, Murdo, Murrough, Murphy (pronounced like 'moor + a + hoo' and 'mer + do' and 'mer + fee')

Murdo is a form of the Gaelic name *Muireachadh*, meaning 'man/hound of the sea', that has also given rise to Murdoch, Murray and possibly Murphy.

Muireann, Muirinn

SEE: **Moran**

Muldoon

SEE: **Maeldun**

Mungo

Mungo was the pet name of St Kentigern and it is said to mean 'dearest friend'. Scholars have worried about the meaning because, although Kentigern was Scottish, Mungo does not seem to be Gaelic. Kentigern's mother was reputed to be a Pictish princess and so we have the possibility that Mungo is actually a Pictish name. Whatever its origins, however, it is an attractive name, made additionally famous by the exploits of the great Scottish explorer, Mungo Park, who led two expeditions to West Africa to trace the source of the River Niger.

SEE: **Kentigern**

Munro

Munro, like a lot of Celtic names, carries in it a history of people and places. The name originated in Ireland as *bun*, 'mouth of' + Roe, a river, possibly meaning 'red'. The 'b' in Gaelic can become 'm' in certain circumstances. For example, *bád* is 'boat' but 'their boat' would be *a mbád*, pronounced like 'a Maud'. The placename was anglicised as Munro or Monroe and used as a surname. The surname was taken to Scotland, where it began to be used as a first name, usually ending in '-o'. Interestingly, many people in Tyrone used to refer to Bundoran as 'Mundoran' and to Buncrana as 'Muncrana', so the tradition of changing the initial sound of 'bun' was still current twenty-five years ago.

Murphy

Murphy is an Irish surname that comes from *muir* + *cath*, 'sea + battle' and probably implying 'warrior from the sea'. It was originally a nickname, then a first name, a surname, and now a given name again.

SEE: **Muireacheadh**

Murray

Murray can be an anglicised form of *Muireachadh*, but it can also come from Moray, in Scotland. Members of the Murray clan often claim that they are descended from Picts who lived in the Moray province. Their skill as warriors goes back at least to the time of the Normans and Sir Andrew Murray fought on the side of William Wallace (Braveheart) at the Battle of Stirling Bridge in 1297. Murray is used quite often as a first name in Scotland, and occasionally in Northern Ireland, where Moray also occurs.

Murtagh (pronounced like 'mer + tah')

Murtagh is an old Gaelic name probably coming from *muirchath* meaning 'sea-battle' and although its popularity waned for many centuries, it is again being used, sometimes in the Irish form and sometimes in the preferred Scottish form, Murdoch.

Mylor

SEE: **Melor**

Naoise, Naoisi, Nyse (pronounced like 'nee + shih')

Naoise was the lover of Deirdre. The meaning of Naoise is uncertain although it may be associated with *nasc*, 'bond'. Naoise fled with Deirdre and his brothers to Scotland to avoid Conchubhar's wrath. They were persuaded to return to Ireland but Naoise was executed by Conchubhar. Traditionally, the name Naoise has been regarded as the Irish equivalent of Noah, meaning 'rest'.

SEE: **Deirdre**

Neal, Neil

These are used both as given names and as surnames. They come from Gaelic Niall. The name may have come from *néal* and meant 'cloud' but it has come to mean 'champion' because of the exploits of Niall of the

Nine Hostages. According to tradition, Niall was a fourth-century king of Tara who gained the throne because of a test. He and his brothers had to find water to quench their thirst. One after the other, the brothers found a well that was guarded by a hideously ugly woman. Before she would allow them to have a drink, she asked for a kiss. Only Niall agreed and, when he had kissed her, she was transformed into the most beautiful woman on earth.

SEE: **Niall**

Nechtan (pronounced like 'neck + tan')

Nechtan may be related to *neach*, 'spirit, mysterious'. He was the husband of Boann. He was the guardian of the well of knowledge and of the hazel trees that grew near it. Nechtan forbade his wife to eat the hazel nuts, but Boann, like Eve, decided to take the risk. The water in the well rose up in anger at the sacrilege and as it chased the fast-running Boann, it turned into the river Boyne.

SEE: **Boann**

Nedeleg, Nodhlag, Nodhlaig, Noel, Nollaig

These names mean Christmas and are thus the equivalent of Noel. They are often given to boys born on 25 December. Nedeleg is the Breton form and the other variants are found in Ireland.

Nelson

Nelson is a blend of Niall, 'champion', and 'son'. It was given a boost as a first name in the nineteenth century after Admiral Nelson's victory over the French fleet at Trafalgar.

SEE: **Niall**

Nessan

Nessan is an example of an Irish name that was virtually extinct but has been revived in the twentieth century. It is possible that it comes from either *an easóg* and means 'stoat' or that it is a male form of Nessa.

SEE: **Nessa**

Nevan, Neven, Nevin, Niven, Nivin

Nevan is related to *naomh*, 'saint, holy one' and was originally a nickname given to a religious person. Neven or Nevenou is honoured in Brittany on 7 March and various forms of the name occur in Scotland, especially as surnames. The Scottish names may come from Norman French and be related to 'nephew'.

Newlyn

This name may mean 'holy pool' or 'new pool'.

SEE: **Navlin**

Niall, Nigel

Niall is sometimes pronounced to rhyme with 'feel' and sometimes with 'nigh + ell'. It is an older version of Neil and probably comes from *niadh*, 'champion'. A famous king of Tara was Niall of the Nine Hostages. No-one is certain how his name arose. It has been suggested that he took hostages from everyone he defeated in battle or, alternatively, that neighbouring clans gave him a hostage to prove that their intentions were peaceful. Nigel comes from Nigellus, a medieval Latin form of Niall.

SEE: **Neala, Neal**

Ninian, Ninn

Ninian was the name of a Celtic saint who helped to spread the Gospel in Scotland. His origin is not certain in that he may be Irish or Welsh or Scottish. Indeed, since he is honoured still in Brittany in both the forms Ninian and Ninn, it is even possible that he was a Breton. It has been suggested that Ninian is a variant of Norman *Vivian* and therefore means 'lively'.

Nissien

Nissien's name means 'peaceful'. He was the brother of Efnissien, 'warlike', and his aim in life was to create peace and tranquillity.

SEE: **Efnissien**

Niven, Nivin

SEE: **Nevan**

Nodhlag, Nodhlaig, Noel, Nollaig

SEE: **Nedeleg**

Nuada (pronounced like 'noo + ah + da')

Nuada was a king of the Tuatha de Danaan, the gods of ancient Ireland. He lost his right hand fighting against invaders and was thus, theoretically, no longer capable of ruling. Diancecht, however, made him a hand of silver that was so perfectly constructed he could even pick up a pinch of salt with it. Diancecht's son, Miach, improved even on that and transplanted a hand of flesh and blood onto Nuada's arm. Nuada's name may be related to modern Irish *nuadhéanta*, 'newly made'.

Nye (pronounced like 'n + eye')

Nye is a short form of Aneurin, the Welsh name that probably comes from Latin Honorius.

SEE: **Aneurin**

Nyse

SEE: **Naoise**

Odhrán, Odran, Oran, Oren, Orin, Orna, Orren, Orrin (pronounced like 'o + ran' or 'or + na')

Oran probably comes from *odhra*, meaning 'dark-haired'. St Oran was Irish but spent much of his life spreading Christianity in Scotland. The name is perhaps more widely known in America than elsewhere because of its use as a character's name in Eugene O'Neill's *Mourning Becomes Electra* (1931). Most of the saints of this name were male but the name seems to be preferred for girls.

Ogilvy (pronounced like 'o + gil + vee')

Ogilvy comes from *ocel fa*, meaning 'high plain' and the Scottish clan that bears this name has had power in Scotland since 1163. The Gaelic version is Ó Giollabhuí.

Oileabhéar, Oilibhéar, Olaf, Oliver

Oileabhéar is an Irish adaptation of Oliver, a name that was introduced into the Celtic communities by the Normans. The name may come from Latin *olivarius*, 'olive tree', a name that would suggest peace and safety. (When Noah's dove returned to the ark with an olive branch in its mouth, Noah knew that the floods had subsided.) It may also be a modification of Olaf, and so mean 'relic of God'. The names Oileabhéar and Plunket(t) became popular in Ireland because of St Oliver Plunket, a bishop of Armagh, who was executed in London in 1681. His head was preserved and kept as a relic in Drogheda.

Oisín, Ossian (pronounced like 'osh + een' or 'oss + ee + an')

Oisín was the son of Fionn MacCool, the leader of the Fianna, and of Saeve or Sive, a goddess. Sive was turned into a deer before her son was born and she brought him up in the forest, giving him a name, *oisín*, that means 'little deer'. When Fionn was hunting, he found the child and recognised him as his son. As Oisín grew up, he became a poet of great distinction and was loved by Niamh, with whom he spent 300 years in the land where time passes slowly and where one never grows old. Yet, in spite of all the delights of Tír na n-Óg, Oisín longed to see his home and friends again. Niamh begged him not to go but his longing for home was so great that she relented. However, when Oisín returned to the scenes of his youth, he discovered that 300 years had passed and that people could hardly remember Fionn and the Fianna. Yeats writes movingly about Oisín's experiences in 'The Wanderings of Oisín'.

Ossian is the form of Oisín used by the Scottish poet, James Macpherson, who published *Fragments of Ancient Poetry Collected in the Highlands of Scotland and Translated from the Gaelic or Erse Language (1760)*. These were followed by *The Poems of Ossian* in 1765. Macpherson's work inspired many of his contemporaries throughout Europe and led to a zeal for the study of all things Celtic.

Olaf, Oliver
SEE: **Oileabhéar**

Onilwyn (pronounced like 'on + ill + win')

Onilwyn is Welsh and was originally a placename meaning 'ash grove'. It has not been widely used in the past but has begun to appear, probably as a result of the surge of interest in Celtic names and traditions.

Oran, Oren, Orin, Orren, Orrin, Odhrán
SEE: **Odhran**

Oscar, Osgar, Osgur

Oscar is usually described as a Scandinavian name deriving from *os + gar*, meaning 'god's spear', and undoubtedly such a meaning may have influenced its spread in Scandinavia. However, Oscar was the name of Oisín's son and almost certainly means 'lover of deer' or 'beloved of deer'. (The Gaelic word for 'deer' is *os*.) The name was made famous by Oscar Wilde whose plays, poetry and short stories remain popular.

Napoleon Bonaparte was so interested in and impressed by James Macpherson's verse, *The Poems of Ossian*, that he called his godson Oscar and this Oscar became King Oscar I of Sweden.

Ossian
SEE: **Oisín**

Owain, Owen, Eoghan, Eoin, Euan, Evan, Ewen

These names are variants of a Celtic name meaning 'well born' or 'yew born'. It is popular in different forms in the different Celtic communities. The Welsh Owain fought against the Angles, the Germanic people who gave their name to England ('Engla + land') and Owain (or Owen) Glyndwr led an uprising against King Henry IV in the fifteenth century.
SEE: **Eoghan, Euan, Tyrone**

Ownie, Owny, Uaine, Uaithne

In Ireland, the popular name Ownie or Owny is usually regarded as a diminutive form of 'Owen', but it is a name in its own right and is related to *uaine*, 'green, verdant' and the phrase *uaine gháire* means 'a peal of laughter'.

Paddy, Páid (pronounced like 'paw + id' or 'paw + idge), Páidín (prounounced like 'paw + idge + een'), Pat, Patsy, Rick

These are abbreviated forms of Padraig and Patrick, both forms of *patricius*, 'of noble birth'.
SEE: **Padraic**

Padarn, Padern, Patern (pronounced like 'pad + darn', 'pad + dern' and 'pat + tern')

Padarn or Paternus was the founder of the Abbey Llanbadarn Fawr (Church of Little Padarn) in Dyfed. Not much is known about him except that his feast day is on 15 April and that he had considerable supernatural powers. Once, when King Arthur appeared to insult the church, Padarn caused the earth to swallow him, up to his neck. Arthur was released only when he begged the old monk for forgiveness. Padarn's name is derived from Latin *pater*, 'father', and means 'fatherly, paternal'. The three forms Padarn, Padern and Patern are found in Brittany, where the sixth-century saint continues to be honoured.

Padraic, Pádraic (pronounced like
'paw + drick'), **Padraig** (pro
nounced like 'paw + drig'),
**Padrig, Padruig, Patric,
Patrice, Patrick**

These names are all derived from the
Latin *patricius*, 'nobly born,
Patrician' although it is possible that
this was a nickname and that the
patron saint of Ireland had a Celtic
name. There are so many legends and
traditions about St Patrick that it is
virtually impossible to be certain
about anything. What is probably
true is that he was born in Britain
around 373 and spoke a Celtic
language, but we cannot be sure
which one. He was captured as a
youth by Irish raiders and forced to
guard sheep. He escaped and trained
as a priest on the Continent and
eventually, after several visions,
made his way back to Ireland, where
he banished the snakes and
converted the population to
Christianity. Patrick's fame spread
far beyond the Celtic regions, and
versions of Patrick are found and
used in virtually all countries.

Patern
SEE: **Padarn**

Parthalán, Parthalon, Partholon
(pronounced like 'parth + a +
lawn'), **Partlan, Partland**

Parthalán was the leader of an
invasion of Ireland. He would be
considered an ecological vandal
today because he is credited with

having cleared the forests from the
central plains of Ireland so that
farming could be carried out. It seems
certain that the name is a form of the
Hebrew Bartholomew, meaning 'son
of Talmai', and Talmai may mean
'ploughman', a name that seems to be
remarkably appropriate for Parthalán.
The name occurs also as the surname
Partlan(d) or MacPartlan and has also
been anglicised as Bartley.
SEE: **Bartley**

Patrick
SEE: **Padraic**

Peada(i)r (pronounced like 'padh +
er')

Peadar is an Irish form of Peter and
thus comes ultimately from Greek
petros, 'rock'. Peadar was a late
borrowing of the name for St Peter.
The Irish also borrowed Petrus from
Latin and Piers from Norman French.
Peadar continues to be one of the
most popular Irish names for a boy.

**Pearce, Pearse, Per, Perig,
Piaras, Pierce, Piers**

The Normans used Piers as a form of
Latin Petrus, which came ultimately
from Greek petros, 'rock'. The Irish
borrowed this as Pearce, Piaras, Pierce
and, less frequently, Piers. The name
was so popular that it was adopted also
as a surname as it is in Padraig Pearse.
The forms Per and Perig continue to be
popular in Brittany.

Penwyn (pronounced like 'pen +
win')

This Welsh name means 'fair head' or 'white head'. It has been suggested that the word 'penguin' comes from the fuller form of this name, *pen + gwyn*, 'head + white'. Groups of Welsh people left Wales to settle in Patagonia, South America, so it is not impossible that they called the strange white-headed bird of the Antarctic 'pen + gwyn' or penguin.

Per, Perig
SEE: **Pearce**

Petroc, Petrog, Petroke (pronounced like 'pet + rock')

These names seem to be Celtic forms of the Greek *petros*, 'rock'. In the sixth century, Petroc founded a monastery in Padstow, Cornwall. He was renowned for his love of animals and his ability to communicate with them. Indeed, when he became a hermit, he communicated only with animals. Petroc would make an excellent patron saint of hunt saboteurs because he used to transform deer into trees so that hunters could not find and kill them. He travelled to Ireland and Brittany and then to Rome, Jerusalem, India and the oceans beyond. Tradition suggests that he lived on an island in what was probably the Indian Ocean for seven years, sustained by one fish.

Phelan, Faolán, Felan (pronounced like 'fail + an' or 'feel + an')

Phelan is an anglicised spelling of Faolán or Felan, a name that comes from a literary word *faol*, meaning

'wolf'. The earliest record of the name seems to be for a follower of Fionn who was so loyal that nothing on earth or in heaven could keep him from his lord.
SEE: **Faolán**

Phelim (pronounced like 'fail + im' or 'feel + im'), Phelimy, Feidhlim, Felim, Feidhlimidh (pronounced like 'fail + im + ee'), Felimy

Phelim is an anglicised form of Feidhlim, a name that comes from feidhil, meaning 'constant, always enduring'. The name has been held by king, poet and warrior and continues to be a popular choice, a choice that has probably been reinforced by the traditional song 'Baidín Fheidhilimí', 'Phelimy's little boat'.

Piaras, Pierce, Piers
SEE: **Pearce**

Plunket(t)

Plunket became popular in Ireland from the 1940s, when moves were made to have Blessed Oliver Plunket canonised.
SEE: **Oileabhéar**

Pól (pronounced like 'pole' or 'poll')

The name of St Paul was borrowed into the Celtic languages as Paulus, which comes from Latin *paulus* and means 'little one'. The form Pól is a modern borrowing. The pronunciation suggests that it was borrowed from French, rather than from English Paul.

Powell (pronounced like 'pow + ill') Powell is a form of *ap* + Hywel, 'son of Hywel'. Its popularity may have been enhanced by the existence of Pwyll, meaning 'prudence'.

Proinsias (pronounced like 'pron + shee + iss')
Proinsias is an Irish form of Francis. The name, which means 'French man' was popularised in Ireland by the Franciscans, whose founder was St Francis of Assisi. The Celts would have been responsive to the stories of St Francis's attitude to birds and animals.
SEE: **Petroc**

Pryce (pronounced like 'price')
Pryce is a form of ap + Rhys, 'son of Rhys'.
SEE: **Reece**

Pwyll (pronounced like 'pow + ill')
Pwyll is a Welsh name meaning 'prudence'. The legendary Pwyll was the lord of Dyfed and the husband of Rhiannon, to whom he was utterly devoted. He was also renowned for his great courtesy, a virtue that was highly regarded by the Celts.

Queran
SEE: **Ciarán**

Quinlan, Quinlevan
Quinlan is most frequently a surname but has begun to be used as a first name. It probably comes from a word such as *caoin dealbhán*, 'gently-

shaped fellow' or *caoine* + *lán*, 'smoothness + full' and implying 'perfection of form'. Quinlevan is a modified form of the same name.

Quinn
Quinn is probably a variant of the name Conn, meaning 'intelligent'. It is an extremely common surname in Northern Ireland, a fact that may have given rise to its current use as a given name.

Rab, Rabbie
SEE: **Riobard**

Rafferty
Rafferty is an Irish surname, related to *rafaireacht*, meaning 'prosperity'. It is occasionally used as a given name, especially when the mother's maiden name is Rafferty.

Raghallaigh, Reilly, Riley (pronounced like 'rah + hal + ee' and 'rye + lee')
These are all forms of a Gaelic adjective, *raghalach*, probably meaning 'courageous, valiant'. The name has begun to be used as a first name although it is still mostly a surname in Ireland and other places where the Irish have settled.

Ramsey
Ramsey is a placename in the Isle of Man and may mean either 'raven's island' or 'ram's island'. The fact that the raven was sacred to the Celts suggests that, in spite of appearances,

the first meaning is the more likely. This name, like Rafferty, is more likely to occur as a surname, although it has been given as a middle name by people with Isle of Man connections.

Randal, Ranulf, Raghnall

Randal was a popular Germanic name and may have meant 'wolf shield'. The Viking form *Ragnvald* seems to have had the additional meaning of 'ruler's advice'. Randal was popular, especially in Northern Ireland, where we find Randalstown, and also in Scotland where 'Lord Randal' is one of the oldest recorded ballads:

> What gat ye for supper, Lord Randal, my son?
> What gat ye for supper, my handsome young man?

Re(a)gan (pronounced like 'ray + gan' or 'ree + gan')

The meaning of Re(a)gan, like the pronunciation, is not fixed. It is likely that it is related to *rí* and thus means 'like a king', or it may come from *ríogach* and mean 'impulsive'. Like a lot of Irish names, it started as a nickname, became a first name, then a surname and is now being used again as a given name.

Réaman(n), Reamon, Redmond (pronounced like 'ray + mon')

These are all Irish versions of the Germanic name *rad + mund*, meaning 'counsellor and protector'. The name was particularly popular in Northern Ireland, where the seventeenth-century Redmond O'Hanlon was such a renowned highwayman that the legend grew up that:

> Twixt Fivemiletown and Crossmaglen
> There are more thieves than honest men.

Rearden, Ríordan (pronounced like 'ree + ir + den')

These names come from *ríoghbhardán* and mean 'royal poet'. It is thus the name of a rank that became a surname and, more recently, a first name. In Irish tradition, a poet was often both highly regarded and feared. Her or his words could immortalise one's memory, either for good or ill.

Reece, Rees, Rhett, Rhys (pronounced like 'hrees' or 'rees')

These names seem to be derived from Welsh *rhys* and to mean 'ardour, passion'. The first two forms are anglicisations of Rhys and Rhett is probably a pet form of the name. Rhett Butler was the hero in *Gone With The Wind* and most filmgoers will remember Clark Gable, playing Rhett, and telling Scarlett O'Hara: 'Frankly, my dear, I don't give a damn.' It is, of course, possible that Margaret Mitchell made up the name, but the use of 'Rh' suggests a Welsh link.

Reilly

SEE: **Raghallaigh**

Rhain (pronounced like 'hra + in')
This name is sometimes confused
with Ryan but, although they are both
Celtic, they are not related. Rhain is
Welsh and means 'lance', a name that
implied 'brave warrior'.

Rhett
SEE: **Reece**

Rhydach, Rhydoch, Riddock
(pronounced like 'hrid + ock')
These names are found in Cornwall
and Devon mainly and probably come
from a Celtic placename, possibly
meaning 'infertile place', or they may
be a Cornish form of *rhydderch* and
mean 'redhead'.

Rhydderch, Rhydderich (pro-
nounced like 'hrid + er + ick')
Rhydderch means 'reddish brown'. It
is a Welsh name and is found also in
'Protheroe', a surname that comes
from *ap + rhydderch*, 'son of the
redhead'. It was sometimes equated
with Roderick, a Germanic name
meaning 'fame and power' because of
the similarity of sound, and
sometimes with Ruadhrí (Rory),
because of the similarity of meaning.
One Welsh Rhydderch was
nicknamed 'the Generous One'
because of the hospitality he offered.
It was said that he had a magic
cauldron that could never be
emptied.

Rhydwyn (pronounced like 'hrid +
win')
Rhydwyn began as a placename,
meaning 'white ford', but it was
adopted as a personal name and has
begun to be used again, as a means of
stressing Welsh identity.

Rhys (pronounced like 'hrees')
SEE: **Reece**

Rick
SEE: **Paddy**

Riddock
SEE: **Rhydach**

Riley
SEE: **Raghallaigh**

Riobard, Riobart, Roibeard, Roibeart, Robert, Rab, Rob
Robert is not a Celtic name but was
taken to Celtic areas by the Normans.
It comes from *hrod + berht*, meaning
'bright fame'. It has become popular
in Ireland, in all its forms, because of
Robert Emmet, who was executed in
1803 and whose speech from the
dock, 'Let no man write my epitaph'
is still regularly recited at festivals in
Ireland. The Scots adopted the name
as Rab and Rabbie, and their
national poet is usually referred to as
Rabbie Burns. Burns adapted Gaelic
themes and melodies and his
lovesongs are among the most
beautiful in any language:

> Till a' the sea gangs dry, my dear,
> And the rocks melt wi' the sun!
> And I will luve thee still, my dear
> While the sands o' life shall run.

Riordan
SEE: **Rearden**

Roarke, Rorke, Rourke, Ruark
(pronounced like 'row + erk' or
'roo + erk')
These are all variants of an Irish
name meaning 'famous ruler'.

Roc, Rock
Roc was a follower of Aengus Óg. His
son was killed by an angry man but
Roc was able to transform his dead
son into a living boar, an animal
sacred to the Celts. The meaning of
Roc is unclear. It may be related to
rocaí, 'person with frizzy hair'. It can
be spelt with a 'k' and has Rocky as a
diminutive form. One of the myths
told in Northern Ireland is how Roc
was turned into a frog and only
allowed to say his name. And from
that day until this, frogs always say:
'Roc, Roc'!

Roddy, Roden, Rody
The Irish adjective *ród* means 'strong'
and has given rise to the name Roden
or Rodin, meaning 'the strong one'.
This name helps to explain the
popularity of Roderick, especially in
its abbreviated form of Rod(d)y.

Rogan
Rogan is one of the many Celtic
names, like Gaelic *ruadh*, meaning
'red-haired'. There are many '-ogan'
surnames in Ireland, Brogan, Hogan,
Logan, Rogan and Wogan, and all but
Wogan occur as given names. Rogan
is extremely popular worldwide and
is found in Zambia and Zimbabwe as
well as Europe, America and
Australia.

Ronan (pronounced like 'ro + nan')
Ronan comes from rón and means
'little seal'. It is found as a first name
in Brittany, Ireland, the Isle of Man
and Scotland. According to Celtic
tradition, sea women could put on
and take off the form of a seal and
could, in certain circumstances, live
with a human man. Their children
would be 'ronans' or 'little seals'.
SEE: **Suibhne**

Rooney
Rooney is an Irish surname that
comes from *ruadh*, 'red', and
probably meant 'redhead' or 'little
redhead'. The surname started to be
used as a first name in the 1940s and
1950s when Mickey Rooney, the
Hollywood actor, was at his most
popular. Traditionally, Rooneys are
very attractive to women:

> The darling of the ladies is the
> Rooney O!

Rorke, Ruarke
SEE: **Roarke**

Rory, Ruadhrí (pronounced like
'ro + ree' and 'roo + ir + ee'),
Ruarí
Rory is extremely popular in Ireland
and Scotland and indeed its
popularity has spread throughout the
English-using world. Rory may come
from *ruadh* and mean 'redhead' or it
may come from *ruadh* + *rí* and mean

'red + king'. It is sometimes used as a diminutive form of Roderick, although the two names are unconnected.

Ross

This name almost certainly comes from Gaelic *ros* meaning 'headland' and found in such places as The Rosses in Donegal or Roscommon, or in Scottish placenames such as Rostrevor. Ross is both a surname and a first name and has been used as a given name since the days of Fionn MacCool when Ros was a warrior and a contemporary of Cúchulainn.

Rowan, Ruad(h)an

Rowan has two main pronunciations. The first syllable may rhyme with 'hoe' or with 'how'. It seems to be a variant of *ruad(h)an* and meant 'little redhead'. It is the name of a number of saints, and since the time of the Vikings, it has been equated with the rowan tree, a tree with bright red berries and sometimes associated with the tree on which Christ was crucified. Ruad(h)an appears in Gaelic mthology as the son of Brigit and Bres and a warrior of great skill and courage.

Roy

Roy almost certainly started in Scotland as a nickname from *ruadh*, meaning 'red', as in Sir Walter Scott's *Rob Roy*. However, it is often thought to come from French *roi*, meaning 'king', and both these meanings cling to the name. Roy was very popular in

the first half of this century and gained an extra spurt in the 1940s when Roy Rogers was the most popular Hollywood cowboy.

Ruad(h)an
SEE: **Rowan**

Ruadhrí
SEE: **Rory**

Rumo, Rumon

Although Rumo or Rumon is regarded as a Cornish saint, whose name seems to be associated with 'red', it is possible that he came from Brittany and may even be one of the saints called Ronan. According to Cornish tradition, Rumo was a bishop who was martyred for his faith.

Ryan

No-one is absolutely certain what Ryan, means although the first syllable probably comes from *rí*, meaning 'king'. It is possible that it means 'little king' or 'royalty'. Ryan is a common surname but it has been used as a first name, especially in America and Australia. The popularity of the Hollywood star, Ryan O'Neal, has assured that Ryan has spread far beyond its original Celtic home.

Sayer

Sayer is a surname that means 'carpenter, craftsman'. It comes from *saor* and the phrase *An Saor* is used for God and often translated as 'the

Great Architect'. The word *saor* is also used to mean 'free', and the anglicised form Sayer began to be used around the time of Irish independence.

SEE: **Saoirse**

Scanlan, Scanlon (pronounced like 'scan + lin')

Scanlan is almost exclusively found as a surname and is said to mean 'attractive, winner of hearts', but it is likely to become more popular as a given name if the vogue for giving children surnames continues.

Sceolan (pronounced like 'skyo + lin')

The link between animals and humans is strong in Gaelic literature, but particularly strong in the extended family of Fionn MacCool. Sceolan's name means 'fleet, agile' and Sceolan was both a hound and Oisín's cousin. His mother was transformed into a hound when she was pregnant and so her child was born a hound.

Scott

Scott is, of course, a variant spelling for Scot, meaning both 'painted warrior' and 'person from Scotland'. The clan known as Scotii actually moved to Scotland from Ireland in the sixth century. The motto of the clan is *Amo*, 'I love', and it has produced many warriors and statesmen, as well as the thirteenth-century Michael, who was a famous alchemist, and the writer, Sir Walter Scott, whose novels helped to ingrain respect for the Gaelic way of life.

Seamus, Seumas, Seumus, Hamish

Seamus is one of the best-known and most widely-used Irish names and yet it is a form of James, meaning 'supplanter'. Seamus has been the given name of many well-known Irishmen, including the Nobel poet laureate, Seamus Heaney. The forms Seumas and Hamish are found mainly in Scotland. Although Seamus cannot claim to be a Celtic name in origin, there is an ancient Irish name Semias that may have encouraged the popularity of Seamus.

SEE: **Hamish**

Seán, Sean, Shane, Shaughan, Shaun, Shawn

These are all forms of the Irish version of John, meaning 'God is gracious' or 'God's gracious gift'. The two main pronunciations, rhyming with 'dawn' and 'Dane', reflect the pronunciations favoured in the south and north of Ireland, respectively. There is a third pronunciation rhyming with 'Dan' but this is less widespread. The name was popularised outside Ireland by the actor Sean Connery. The form Shane is still used in Northern Ireland in memory of the sixteenth-century Shane O'Neill, whose forces defeated Elizabeth I's in Tyrone.

Seanán, Senan, Sezni, Shannon, Sionán, Zenan

These variants are all related to *sean*, 'old' and all mean 'old, wise' and they are becoming popular, especially in the anglicised spelling 'Shannon'. There was a sixth-century Irish saint called Senan, who was renowned throughout the Celtic world and who may be the source of Breton Sezni and Cornish Zenan. The Cornish also had a female saint, 'Sancta Senan' or 'Sancta Senara' but little is known about her. The name could apply equally to a man or a woman because it was really a term of respect, like 'senator'.

Semias (pronounced like 'shem + ee + iss')

According to Irish tradition, Semias was one of the wisest people who ever lived. The meaning of his name is unclear but it may be related to *séaghainn*, meaning 'distinguished, accomplished', or possibly even to *simeasóg*, 'little shamrock'. He had a cauldron of knowledge and wisdom and anyone who ate or drank from the cauldron had access to all the knowledge of the past and the future.

Senan
SEE: **Seanán**

Seosamh (pronounced like 'sho + soo', or 'sho + siv')

Seosamh is the Irish form of Joseph, a Hebrew name meaning 'God shall add'. Joseph was the husband of the Blessed Virgin Mary and the stepfather of Jesus. He was thus given special respect by the early Celtic church. Later, he became the patron saint of workmen.

Setanta
Setanta was the original name of Cúchulainn.
SEE: **Cúchulainn**

Sezni
SEE: **Seanán**

Shane
SEE: **Seán**

Shanley
Shanley is mainly an Irish surname. It comes from *sean laoch* and its meaning of 'venerable warrior' implies that it is appropriate as a given name.

Shannon
SEE: **Seanán**

Shantaigh, Shantigh (pronounced like 'shantee')

Shantaigh is a form of Seán, John, used as a diminutive originally but now often taken as a name in its own right.

Shaughan, Shaun
SEE: **Seán**

Shaw
Shaw is an Anglo-Saxon name meaning 'grove', but it has begun to be used as a first name, partly as a result of the popularity of the Irish play-wright, George Bernard Shaw. Some Irish people claim that 'Shaw' is a modified form of 'Shea'. There is also a Scottish clan called Shaw whose Gaelic name is Mac Ghille Sheathanaigh, also sometimes anglicised as Chattan.

Shawn
SEE: **Seán**

Shea (pronounced like 'shay')
Shea and O'Shea come from an old Irish given name, *Sé*, meaning 'like a hawk' and implying 'graceful, keen-sighted, courageous, strong, free'.

Sheridan
Sheridan is an Irish surname that has begun to be used as a given name. Its meaning is uncertain although it may include *síor*, meaning 'eternal', and *dán*, meaning 'treasure, poem'. The Anglo-Irish writer Sheridan Le Fanu is one example.

Sinclair
Sinclair is so widely regarded as a Scottish name that it is not always realised that it comes from 'Saint Claire' and thus means 'holy light'. The Scottish Sinclairs came from St Claire-sur-Elle in Normandy. A William Sinclair carried Robert the Bruce's heart to the Holy Land.

Sionán
SEE: **Seanán**

Somerled, Somhairle, Sorley, Summerlad
The Irish adopted the Viking name *sumarlithr*, meaning 'summer traveller' and it is found in Ireland, Scotland and the Isle of Man as the surname MacSorley, 'son of the summer traveller'. The Scots also preserve the name in Somerled and Summerlad, the second being a folk etymology. The name Sorley has begun to be used as a given name.

Stewart, Stuart
The origin of these names goes back to the Middle Ages, when Sir Walter Fitz-Allan was made the High Steward of Scotland by King David I. The Stewarts or Stuarts, as the French called them, married well and fourteen of them have ruled, either in Scotland or in England. One of the best-known of these was Mary Stuart, Queen of Scots, who was executed by Elizabeth I.

Strachan, Struan (pronounced like 'strawn' or 'strah + han')
Strachan is a Scottish surname meaning 'poet'. It is occasionally used as a first name, as is the variant Struan.

Suibhne, Sweeney, Sweeny (pronounced like 'swiv + nee' and 'swee + nee')
There is debate about the meaning of Suibhne. It may mean 'hero' or it may be related to *subhuigh*, 'exhilarate'. There is, however, no debate about the character known as Suibhne Gelt or Mad Sweeney. According to legend, Sweeney was a seventh- century king of Ireland. He got angry with Saint Ronan for his over-zealous ringing of church bells and threw the saint's prayerbook into the lake. St Ronan cursed the king, who is reputed to have lost his wits. How- ever, if we view him with ecological eyes, we may think that he found freedom in his

'madness'. He gave up his job, went to live in the treetops, flying south with the birds in winter and living on what nature provided. Sweeney regained his wits sufficiently to find a saint who gave him the last rites before he died.

Sulian, Sulien (pronounced like 'soo + lee + en')

Sulian is occasionally used in Brittany as a form of Julian, a name that comes from Latin Julius, whose most famous bearer was Julius Caesar. The Welsh name Sulien is occasionally used for Julian but comes from Welsh and is said to mean 'sun-born' or 'summer baby'.

Sullivan

Sullivan, which comes from *súil*, 'eye', is related to *súilaibí*, meaning 'keen-eyed' and could easily become a given name. At the moment it is used almost always as a surname.

Summerlad
SEE: **Somerlad**

Sweeney, Sweeny
SEE: **Suibhne**

Tadhg (pronounced like the first syllable in 'tiger')

Tadhg is an Irish name meaning 'poet'. It is sometimes pronounced 'tad' in America and written as Tadd or, occasionally, Todd, although these are unrelated names, the first meaning 'father' and the second 'fox'.

Many Irish people translate Tadhg as Tim, thus equating it with Timothy, meaning 'God's honour'.

Tafydd
SEE: **Dai**

Taliesin (pronounced like 'tal + ee + sin')

Taliesin is one of the better-known Welsh names, thanks to Taliesin's role in literature. The name is Welsh for 'shining brow' and Taliesin is often credited with being one of the greatest poets who ever lived.

Tanguy, Tangwyn (pronounced like 'tang + gee' and 'tang + win')

Tangwyn is a Welsh name related to *tangnefedd*, 'peace' + *gwyn*, 'pure', and meaning 'blessed peace'. It seems to be related to the Breton name Tanguy or Tangi, whose feast day is celebrated on 18 November.

Tearlach (pronounced like 'tar + loch')

Tearlach and Searlas are both used in Ireland as forms of Charles, introduced by the Normans and meaning 'man'. The name became especially popular after AD 800, when Charlemagne was crowned Emperor of the Holy Roman Empire. The form of Tearlach has been influenced by Turloch.
SEE: **Turloch**

Ter(r)ence, Torrance

Ter(r)ence is a popular Irish name, derived from Latin terentius and probably meaning 'polished'. It is the name of the Classical dramatist, Marcus Terentius and there are several saints who bear the name. The name Torrance occurs in Ireland and is possibly a blend of Torin and Ter(r)ence.

Thurloe, Thurlow
SEE: **Turloch**

Tiernan (pronounced like 'tee + ir + nan')
Tiernan and Tierney both come from *tighern*, 'lord' and Tiernan is often translated as 'lord of the household, chief'. Both names occur widely as surnames and are also used as given names for sons.

Tierney (pronounced like 'tee + ir + nee')
Tierney was originally a form of *tighern*, meaning 'lord'. It is closely related to Tiernan but usually considered a separate name. There was a sixth-century Ulster saint called Tighernach or Tierney. He had the privilege of being baptised by St Brigid, a fact that supports the claim that women often played priestly roles in the old Celtic church.

Tole, Tuathal, Tully (pronounced like 'tole', 'tooh + hill' and 'tull + ee')
The Irish word *tuathal* means 'leader or prince of the people'. It has been used as a nickname and a surname rather than a given name, but it is attractive in both form and meaning and so could be about to become popular in the Gaelic form Tuathal.

Tomás (pronounced like 'tom + moss')
Tomás is clearly a form of Thomas, a biblical name meaning 'twin'. This form of the name was and is particularly popular in Northern Ireland and was the name of an Archbishop of Armagh.

Tone
Theobald Wolfe Tone was a United Irishman executed for his part in the 1798 Rebellion against the English. His memory is honoured by many parents who have named their sons Tone. In Irish Gaelic, *Tón* or *Tóin* can be used for Anthony, a name that may mean 'of inestimable value'. Tóin is unlikely to be used in Ireland as most parents know that it means 'backside'!

Torin (pronounced like 'tor + in')
Torin is often thought to be an anglicisation of Gaelic *torfhinn*, meaning 'chief' or *tóirneach*, meaning 'thunder' and the link with Thor, the Viking god of thunder is clear. The name is also found in the region of Cornwall and in the Isle of Man, suggesting that it was once more widely used.

Torrence
SEE: **Ter(r)ence**

Tostig (pronounced like 'toss + tig' or 'tuss + tig')
This Welsh name means 'pointed' and suggests 'warrior'.

Trefor, Trevor

Like many Celtic names, this one has been used as a placename, a surname and now, almost exclusively, as a given name. It comes from Welsh *tref* + *for*, meaning 'large settlement' and the two forms of the name are used. Irrespective of spelling, the Welsh tend to pronounce the name with a central '-f-' but others prefer the '-v-' pronunciation. The word *tref* ('settlement'), originally meant 'farmstead' and is related to the Irish Gaelic *treabhadh*, 'ploughing'.

Tremaine, Tremayne

According to Cornish tradition, this surname means 'rock settlement' and so may, originally, have been associated with a lighthouse. As Cornish nationalism grows, names like Tremaine are more widely used in the region.

Trevelyan

Many lovely Cornish names have been preserved as surnames. The ones that begin with *tre-* include the meaning of 'settlement'. This one means 'settlement of the bright one'. It has recently begun to be used as a given name.

Tristan, Tristram

Tristan's name occurs in various forms but it is likely that they have all been influenced by French *triste*, 'sad'.
SEE: **Drustan, Isolt**

Tuathal

SEE: **Tole**

Tudor

Tudor was originally a Welsh surname, often written *Tewdwr* and thought to be related to *twt*, 'neat'. Owen Tudor married the widow of Henry V and his grandson Henry Tudor defeated Richard III in 1485 and became King Henry VII of ngland. Many people equate Tudor with Theodore, a name that means 'gift of God'.

Tully

SEE: **Tole**

Turloch, Turlough, Turlow (pronounced like 'ter + loch' and 'toor + loch')

Turlough is an Irish name possibly meaning 'initiator' or 'shaped like Thor', the Viking god of thunder. It was the name of the poet Turlough O'Carolan, who wrote in Irish Gaelic and who has been translated by Austin Clarke.

Tyrone (pronounced like 'tir + own' in Ireland and 'tie + rone' elsewhere)

Tyrone is the name of a county in Northern Ireland. It means 'land of Eoghan, land of the noble'. It was the given name of the Hollywood actor, Tyrone Power and his director cousin, Tyrone Guthrie. It has been popular, especially in America, since the 1950s but County Tyrone is now producing its own Tyrones.
SEE: **Tyrona**

Early Celtic alphabets did not make use of the letters V, X, Y or Z and so, we do not find many examples of traditional names beginning with these letters.

Uaine, Uaithne
SEE: **Ownie**

Uilliam (pronounced like 'wil + ee + am')
Uilliam is occasionally used as an Irish form of William, but Liam is preferred.
SEE: **Liam**

Uinseann (pronounced like 'win + shan')
Uinseann is the Irish equivalent of Vincent, which means 'conquering'. There are several St Vincents but St Vincent de Paul, who founded orders to care for the poor and the sick, is still respected in Ireland.

Ultán (pronounced like 'ool + tawn')
Ultán means 'Ulsterman' and it is the name of several of the many saints from Ulster. A famous seventh-century St Ultán went to France and was renowned throughout Europe for his piety and simplicity.

Urien (pronounced like 'your + ian')
Urien occurs both in Wales and Brittany and seems to mean 'town dweller'. The name may have been influenced by Latin *urbs*, 'city', or Hebrew *Uri*, meaning 'light'.

Urquhart (pronounced like 'irk + art')
The Gaelic form of this Scottish clan name is Urchurdan, related to urchar, 'throw a missile'. If we are to believe Sir Thomas Urquhart, who died in 1660, he was the 143rd in direct descent from Adam. This is the same Sir Thomas who translated Rabelais and who is reputed to have died laughing.

Usna (pronounced like 'oosh + na')
Usna was an Ulster chieftain and his name seems to be related to *uisinn*, 'temple of the head'. Deirdre was married to Naoise, one of his three sons (his other sons were Ainle and Ardan), and there is a place in Westmeath called Uisneach Hill.
SEE: **Deirdre**

Vaughan (pronounced like 'vawn')
Vaughan derives from the Welsh adjective *bychan*, meaning 'small'. In Welsh, as in all the Celtic languages, 'v' is sometimes the pronunciation of a 'b'. (The phenomenon is known as 'mutation'.) The name is found as a surname and is currently popular also as a given name.

Visant (pronounced like 'vee + san')
Visant is a Breton form of Vincent,

from Latin *vincens*, meaning 'conquering'. St Vincent de Paul, the French saint, was popular in all Catholic communities.
SEE: **Uinseann**

Vivian, Vivien
SEE: **Béibhinn**

Vychan (pronounced like 'vich + an')
Vychan is a Welsh name derived from *bychan*, 'small'. It is a less widely used variant of Vaughan.

Wallace, Walsh, Wallis, Welch, Welsh
Wallace and its various forms comes from an Anglo-Saxon word *wealh*, meaning 'foreigner'. The Latin equivalent *Wallensis* was used in Scotland to describe the Celts, especially those who lived in the Strathclyde area. Perhaps the best-known Wallace was William Wallace or Braveheart, who lived from 1274-1305 and whose guerrilla techniques were extremely successful against the English, until he was betrayed and executed. The motto of the Wallaces is *Pro Libertate*, 'For Liberty'. Wallace has been popular as a first name, especially among people of Scottish ancestry. It is likely to become even more popular after the success of the Mel Gibson film, *Braveheart*.

Waylon, Weylin
These names seem to be Celtic although their precise meaning is unclear. They are said to mean 'son of the wolf'. The

spelling of Waylon and its popularity may have been influenced by the Anglo-Saxon name Wayland.

Welch, Welsh
SEE: **Wallace**

Wynford
Wynford is probably an anglicised form of *gwyn* + *ior*, Gwynfor, meaning 'fair lord'.
SEE: **Gwynfor**

Wynn
Wynn is quite a popular Welsh name, a variant of *gwyn*, 'fair, holy'.

Yestin (pronounced like 'yes + tin')
Yestin is used in Welsh as the equivalent of Justin, meaning 'fair, just'. St Justin was a second-century theologian.

Yollan, Yolland
SEE: **Iollan**

Yorath
SEE: **Iorweth**

Yorwin, Yorwyn
SEE: **Iorwyn**

Ynyr (pronounced like 'in + ir')
Ynyr is a Welsh form of Latin Honorius, meaning 'honour'.

Zenon (pronounced like 'zen + on')

Zenan
SEE: **Senan**

INDEX

BRETON

CORNISH

IRISH

ISLE OF MAN

SCOTTISH

Abloec 76
Adaryn 12
Adeon 76
Aderyn 12
Aelhaeran 77
Aeronwen 12
Afagdu 77
Aled 79
Aleid 79
Aleine (Eleyne) 14
Alhern (Alhaern) 79, 77
Alun 78, 79
Amatheon 79
Anarawd 79
Anchoret 15
Aneira 15
Aneurin 80
Angharad 15
Angwyn 80, 123
Annowre 15
Ardal 81
Ardanata 16
Arianrhod 17
Arthfael 81
Arthur 81, 85
Auryn 82
Austell 82
Avallach 83
Awena 18

Banadel 83, 87
Banier 83
Bard 83
Barinthus 83, 84, 116
Barris 84, 116
Bedivere 85
Bedwyr 85
Belvedere 85
Benedalor 83, 87
Berwin 85
Bevan 85, 113, 19, 20
Bevin 85, 113, 19, 20
Bladud 85
Blodeuwedd 21
Blodwen 21; 20
Boadicea 21, 89
Boudicca 21
Bowen 86, 113, 146
Brangwyn 24, 22
Branwalader 85, 87

Branwen 22, 24
Brecon 87
Bregon 87
Brenda 22, 88
Brendan 88, 135
Breward 85
Brewin 85
Briallen 23
Briana 23, 88
Brice 88
Brisen 23
Brongwyn 24, 22
Bronwen (Bronwyn) 24, 22
Bryce 88
Brychan 87, 89
Bryn 89, 24
Brynna 24, 89
Bryony 24, 89

Caddell 90
Caddock 90
Cadeyrn 90
Cado 90
Cadoc 90
Cadog 90
Cadwallader 90
Caeribormeith 24
Calidore 91
Camber 92
Camden 92
Caradoc 93
Caradog 93
Carannog 93
Carantoc 93
Carantog 93
Caronwyn 25
Caryl (Caryll) 25
Carys 25
Caswallawn 94
Cecil 95
Ceinlys 26
Ceiridwen 26
Ceri 27
Cerian 27
Ceridwen 26
Cerwyn 95
Cigfa 27
Cledwin 96
Conway 99
Conwy 99

Cordelia 28
Creiddylad 29
Creirwy 29
Crisiant 29
Culhwch 101
Cyhyreath 30
Cynog 92, 101

Dafydd 102, 101
Dai 102
David 102, 103
Dawe 103
Delbchaem 32
Delebchaim 32
Delwin 32
Delwyn 32
Derryth 33, 31
Devin 105, 33
Dewi (Dewey) 102, 105
Dillon 105, 108
Dilys 33, 32
Diwrnach 106
Docco 103, 106
Dochau 103, 106
Docwina 103, 106
Don 34, 30
Donwenna 34, 35
Dwyn 35
Dwynwen 35
Dylan 108
Dyrnwch 106, 109

Edryd 109
Efnissien 110, 144
Eilwen 37
Eiros 110
Eirwen 37
Elen 37
Elfed 111
Elidr 111, 79
Elisud 111
Ellidor 111, 79
Ellis 111
Elphin 111
Eluned 38
Elvi 112
Elwa 38
Elwin 112
Elwy 38
Emlyn 112

GIRLS

BOYS

Hogan 124
Hugh 124
Huw 124
Hywell (Howell) 124

Iagan 110, 124
Iain 124, 113
Ian 124, 113
Iarnan 113, 125
Idris 125
Idwal 125
Ieuan 124, 113, 125
Ifor 125
Illtud 125
Illtyd 125
Inir 125
Innes 125
Innis 125
Inyr 125
Iobhar 125
Iollan 126
Iorweth 126
Iorwyn 126
Irwin 109
Ith 126
Ithel 126
Iuchar 126
Iucharba 126
Ivi 125, 126
Ivor 125, 126
Iwan 124, 113, 126

Jacut 127
Jago 127
Jagu 127
Jakez 127, 154
Jared 127, 119
Jarret 127, 119
Jegu 127
Job 127, 155
Jonty 127, 154
Jos 127, 155

Ka (Kai) 91, 127
Kadec (Kadeg) 90, 127
Kain 127, 96
Kanack 92
Kane 127, 96
Karantec (Karantoc) 93, 128
Karl 94, 128
Kary 128, 93
Kay 91, 127
Kaye 91

Ke (Kaie) 91
Kean 128, 96, 51
Keane 128, 96
Kearney 94, 128
Keegan 128, 110
Keelan 128, 51, 25
Keeley 128, 51
Keelin 128, 51, 25
Keenan 128, 96, 52
Keir 128
Keiron 96, 128
Keith 128
Keller 128
Kelly 128, 52
Kelvin 129
Kendrick 129
Kenn 129
Kennedy 129
Kenneth 129, 92
Kent 127
Kentigern 129
Kermit 130, 105
Kermode 130, 105
Kerry 130, 52, 27
Keverne 130, 93
Kevin (Kevan) 130, 93
Kew (Kewe) 124, 130, 52
Key 130, 91, 127
Kiaran 96, 53
Kieran 96, 130
Kieran 130, 96
Kieron 96, 130
Killian 96, 130
Kinnell 130
Kinnock 92, 131
Kolman 97, 131
Konan 98, 131
Kyle 131
Kynon 131, 98

Labhras 131
Labraid 131
Lach 131
Lachlann 131
Lance 131
Lancelot 131
Lann 132
Lanval 132
Laoghaire 134, 132
Launcelot 131
Lear 132, 43
Leary 134, 132

Lee 132
Leigh 132
Lennon 132
Lennox 132
Liam 132, 123
Lir 132, 43, 133
Lleufer 133
Llew 133
Llewellyn 133
Lloyd 133
Llywelyn 133
Lochinvar 133, 131
Lochlan(n) 131, 133
Loegaire 134
Loeiz 134
Logan 134
Loic 134
Loig 134
Lorcan 134
Lorcán 134
Lugh 134, 133
Lughaidh 134

Macaulay 134
Macauley 134
Mack 135
Mackenzie 135
Madeg 135
Madoc 135
Mael 135
Maelduine 135
Maeldún 135
Magee 136
Magnus 136
Mailyr 138, 136
Maines 136
Malachy 136
Malcolm 136, 97
Malo 135, 137
Malvin 137, 57, 138, 139
Manannan 137
Manawyddan 137
Manus 136, 137
Maodez 137
Maolíosa 137, 57
Mark 137
Marmaduke 137, 135
Marrac 137, 135
Marvin 138, 139, 141
Math 138
Maudez (Modez) 137
Mawes 137, 138

Maxen 138, 136
Maxwell 138
McGee 136, 138
McGhie 136, 138
Meala 135
Meilir 138
Meilyr 138
Mel 135, 138
Melan 138
Melar 138
Mellanus 138
Melor 138, 139, 144
Melorus 139, 144
Melville 139
Melvin 139
Melvyn 139
Meredith 139, 58
Meriadeg 139
Meriadoc 139
Merlin 139
Merlyn 139, 58
Merven 138, 139
Mervin 138, 139
Mervyn 139
Miach 140
Micheál 140
Midhir 140
Mikael 140
Milo 140
Mitch 140
Mitchel 140
Mitchell 140
Moran 140
Moray 141, 142
Morgan 141, 60
Morvan 138, 139, 141
Muireachadh 141
Muireann 140, 141
Muirinn 140, 141
Muldoon 135, 141
Mungo 141, 129
Munro 141
Murdo 141
Murphy 142, 141, 61
Murray 142
Murrough 141
Murtagh 142
Mylor 139, 144

Nelson 143
Naoise 142, 32
Naoisi 142, 32

Neal 142, 143
Nechtan 143, 21
Nedeleg 143
Neil 142, 143
Nessan 143, 62
Nevan 143
Neven 143
Nevin 143
Niall 143, 61, 142
Nigel 143, 61, 142
Ninian 144
Ninn 144
Nissien 144, 110
Niven 143, 144
Nivin 143, 144
Nodhlagh 143, 144
Nodhlaig 143, 63, 144
Noel 143, 144
Nollaig 143, 63, 144
Nuada 144
Nye 144, 80
Nyse 142, 32, 144

Odhrán 144, 64, 146
Ogilvy 145
Oileabhéar 145
Oilibhéar 145
Oisín 145
Olaf 145
Oliver 145
Onilwyn 145
Oran 144, 64, 146
Orin (Orrin) 144, 64, 146
Orna 144, 64
Oscar 146
Osgar 146
Osgur 146
Ossian 145, 146
Owain 146, 113, 159
Owen 113, 146, 159
Ownie 146
Owny 146

Padarn 146
Paddy 146, 147, 65
Padern 146
Padraic 147
Pádraic 147
Padraig 147
Padrig 147
Padruig 147
Páid 146, 147

Parthalán 147, 84
Parthalon 147, 84
Partholon 147, 84
Partlan 147, 84
Partland 147, 84
Pat 146, 147, 65
Patern 146, 147
Patric 147
Patrice 147
Patrick 147
Patsy 146, 147, 65
Peadair 147
Peadar 147
Pearce 147
Pearse 147
Penwyn 147
Per 147, 148
Perig 147, 148
Petroc 148
Petrog 148
Petroke 148
Phelan 114, 148
Phelim 148
Phelimy 148
Piaras 147, 148
Pierce 147, 148
Piers 147, 148
Plunket 148, 145
Plunkett 148, 145
Pól 148
Powell 149
Proinsias 149, 148
Pryce 149, 150
Pwyll 149

Quay 91
Queran 96, 149
Quinlevin 149
Quinlan 149
Quinn 149

Rab 151, 149
Rabbie 151, 149
Rafferty 149
Raghallaigh 149
Raghnal 150
Raghnall 150
Ramsey 149
Randal 150
Ranulf 150
Reagan 150
Réaman 150